AF411548

Female Subjectivity in African American Women's Narratives of Enslavement

Female Subjectivity in African American Women's Narratives of Enslavement

Beyond Borders

Lynette D. Myles

FEMALE SUBJECTIVITY IN AFRICAN AMERICAN WOMEN'S NARRATIVES OF ENSLAVEMENT
Copyright © Lynette D. Myles, 2009.

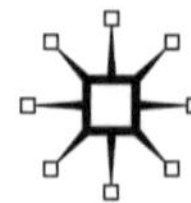

First published in 2009 by
PALGRAVE MACMILLAN®
in the United States—a division of St. Martin's Press LLC,
175 Fifth Avenue, New York, NY 10010.

Where this book is distributed in the UK, Europe and the rest of the world,
this is by Palgrave Macmillan, a division of Macmillan Publishers Limited,
registered in England, company number 785998, of Houndmills,
Basingstoke, Hampshire RG21 6XS.

Palgrave Macmillan is the global academic imprint of the above companies
and has companies and representatives throughout the world.

Palgrave® and Macmillan® are registered trademarks in the United States,
the United Kingdom, Europe and other countries.

ISBN: 978–0–230–61593–9

Library of Congress Cataloging-in-Publication Data

Myles, Lynette D.
    Female subjectivity in African American women's narratives of
    enslavement : beyond borders / Lynette D. Myles.
        p. cm.
    Includes bibliographical references and index.
    ISBN 978–0–230–61593–9 (alk. paper)
    1. American fiction—African American authors—History and
    criticism. 2. American fiction—Women authors—History and criticism.
    3. African American women in literature. 4. Identity (Psychology) in
    literature. 5. Consciousness in literature. 6. Subjectivity in literature.
    7. Place (Philosophy) in literature. 8. Space and time—Psychological
    aspects. 9. African American women—Race identity. 10. African
    American women—Psychology. I. Title.

PS153.N5M95 2009
813.009—dc22   2009006234

A catalogue record of the book is available from the British Library.

Design by Newgen Imaging Systems (P) Ltd., Chennai, India.

First edition: November 2009

10 9 8 7 6 5 4 3 2 1

Printed in the United States of America.

To Lynn, Natalie, and Tres
and
to the memory of
Eugenia C. DeLamotte (1951–2005)

CONTENTS

Acknowledgments   ix

1   Introduction: Places, Borders, and Margins—
    Locating a Black Feminist Model of Interpretation   1

2   Black Female Movement: Conceptualizing Places
    of Consciousness for Black Female Subjectivity   11

3   Location, Female Autonomy, and Identity in
    Pauline Hopkins's *Contending Forces*   51

4   At the Crossroads of Black Female Autonomy, or
    Digression as Resistance in *Quicksand* and *The Street*   83

5   *Praisesong for the Widow*: Crossing Location and
    Space toward Female Consciousness and Wholeness   117

6   Space and Time: The Interdependency of History,
    Identity, and Survival in Octavia Butler's *Kindred*   147

7   Conclusion   165

Notes   173

Bibliography   183

Index   191

ACKNOWLEDGMENTS

I wish to thank Arizona State University Division of Graduate Studies for the Dissertation Fellowship that enabled me to complete my dissertation. I am also thankful for the support from the Department of English and African and African American Studies Program.

In addition, I would like to acknowledge the professors who encouraged and supported me. I am grateful to my dissertation committee chair Professor Neal A. Lester who provided advice and support. I am thankful to Professor Keith Miller for his support, encouragement, and enthusiasm. I am appreciative of Professor Lisa M. Anderson for her help and assistance. I am deeply grateful to the late Professor Eugenia C. DeLamotte who helped shape this project and provided inspiration and support to my ideas. Also, I like to thank professors O. M. Brack, Patricia Neff, Leanor Boulin Johnson, and Angelita D. Reyes for their support during my graduate studies.

I also owe a large debt of thanks to mentor Professor DoVeanna Fulton Minor, University of Alabama, Tuscaloosa, who has been immensely supportive and helpful; for all the many rich, wide-ranging discussions, I am grateful. For inspiring and supporting me, I like to thank Professor Stanlie James. I want to also thank Professors Ayanna Thompson, Alyssa Robillard, and Olga I. Davis for their encouragement and support.

I am also grateful to my students in my African American Literature courses at Arizona State University who helped me to see things differently and with whom I had delightful dialogue. Thanks to Abena Hinds, Natalie Vie, Zoe Sarabo, Robert Casey, Billy Cioffi, Adelina Franciotti, Michael Kato, Donnell Phillips, Michael Mabry, Lafayette Newsome, and Alia Mackins.

For providing me love, support, and inspiration, I would like to thank my family, especially Lynn, Natalie, Tres' and Alex. I want to also thank Ralph, Rose, Nicoly, and Zachary. And I am grateful to my friend Jai Park and sister friends Demetria Baker, Norma Kenner, Norma Moore, and Veronica Njeri-Imani who provided me friendship and support.

1

Introduction: Places, Borders, and Margins—Locating a Black Feminist Model of Interpretation

Therefore, she was forced to begin a...pilgrimage—a hunt for the means to help her breast the social tide.

—Pauline Hopkins[1]

The psychological, moral, spiritual, and intellectual energies expended in the engagement with the forces of violence are generated by an anxiety about boundaries: those that shut the protagonist off from the world, those that shut the protagonist in, and those that separate the individual self from something that is Other.

—Eugenia DeLamotte[2]

Spaces can be real and imagined. Spaces can tell stories and unfold histories. Spaces can be interrupted, appropriated, and transformed through artistic and literary practice.

—bell hooks[3]

In the above passage from Pauline Hopkins' *Contending Forces* (1900), the narrator illuminates the course for Mrs. Willis and other black women at the turn of the century in positioning themselves as resourceful and proficient true women. The excerpt from DeLamotte reflects the tireless efforts of women in fighting against female oppression, particularly the barriers that cut off and intrude upon black women's existence, while hooks's passage speaks to the usefulness of space for change and renewal. The fact that these passages center on women and place shows the concern of employing space as transformative sites for female renewal. From the publication of Maria W. Stewart's essays and speeches in 1831 to Sherley Anne William's *Dessa Rose* (1986), locating places to reclaim black female agency as well as implementing change are dominant themes for African American women writers. Essays on and narratives of female enslavement and resistance explicitly demonstrate black women coming to terms with their lesser positions in hegemonic society. Given the impact of the damaging effect of the assigned position that Nanny in Zora Neale Hurston's *Their Eyes Were Watching God* (1937) describes as "mules of the world" (14), it is not surprising that African American women have worked assiduously to change the position that keeps them silent and powerless.

LOCATIONS FOR CHANGE

Against the backdrop of black female resistance, bell hooks, in "Choosing the Margin as a Space of Radical Openness," considers spaces where blacks have greater possibilities for change. Transformation, as hooks suggests, takes place in settings where blacks can resist and move against oppressive boundaries set by race, sex, and class domination (*Yearning* 145). However, in moving "out of one's place," hooks makes the point that the oppressed need to consider and recognize "the realities of choice and location" as marginalized people (hooks 145). As hooks understands, the choice or decision to move out of places of oppression is a critical one.

For African American women, the choice to move from or remain in subjugated places determines black women's response to existing cultural practices of female oppression and their willingness to envision new alternatives and radical ways of living (145). A change of black women's condition indicates moving from a place of complacency—on the margin—to a site outside hegemonic domains of power, or away from the center of its discourse. However, hooks' argues that the location for radical change is a place found on the margin where one can speak from a voice of resistance and where one can say no to the colonizer. It is that inclusive space on the margin, she says, where the oppressed can recover and also where they "move in solidarity to erase the category colonized/colonizer" (152).

In this respect, hooks's comments about politics of location provide a viable frame for my focus. This study considers five female narratives of enslavement—Pauline Hopkins's *Contending Forces* (1900), Nella Larsen's *Quicksand* (1928), Ann Petry's *The Street* (1946), Paule Marshall's *Praisesong for the Widow* (1983), and Octavia Butler's *Kindred* (1979)—through the critical lens of hooks's assertions about places of location for black female resistance and transformation. Recognizing that visibility and voice constitute the essence of selfhood, African American women, figuratively and literally, have searched for new "spaces" to articulate their existence away from female oppression and exploitation. Such sites and locations are not those found on the margin of white patriarchal society, as hooks speculates. Instead, spaces for resistance are found in regions outside these ideologies—regions that allow women to take control of their lives. Specifically, they are places where black women create a distinct language that articulates their unique existence. In the process of recreating their histories, African American women writers locate black female realities and affirm new identities in places that broaden their lives rather than sites that restrict them on the margins.[4]

Drawing on the works of black feminist literary and cultural scholars and critics, this study demonstrates how writers promote separate spaces and locations for a changed female consciousness and development. Specifically, the works here offer explanations of how personal change occurs in spaces outside the ones that radically limit black female action. As Claudia Tate makes clear,

> This type of change...occurs because the heroine recognizes, and more importantly respects her inability to alter a situation....This is not to imply that she is completely circumscribed by her limitations. On the contrary, she learns to exceed former boundaries but only as a direct result of knowing where they lie. (xxiv)

Tate's assertion is realized by the black female characters considered in this study who recognize the limits placed on their lives and the positions having been assigned to them by holders of power. In fact, in coming to female consciousness[5] after crossing borders of difference, black women come to understand how hegemony works in suppressing black women's history and their very existence on the margins of society.

Investigating the crossing of borders for female subjectivity, this study raises the following questions: What effect do boundaries and places have on African American women's identities? How does location connect to black women's autonomy and female subjectivity? How do space and place open new landscapes for African American women's gender consciousness? Are boundaries constructed to restrict or to broaden the scope of black women's lives? Though borders are frequently thought of as enclosing and limiting movement within particular localities, in this study, spaces and boundaries take a new and different meaning, particularly for African American women. In fact, this study shows *when* and *how* black women use and cross spaces and borders to move from marginal positions to realize possibilities for change.

With a close examination of spaces or places as sites of resistance, this study illustrates when and how black women cross physical, psychological, and metaphorical boundaries in order to define their lives outside racially and patriarchally biased orders that relegate them to invisible sexual objects. An investigation of crossing "borders" assesses the impetus behind African American women radically transgressing into different landscapes and answers how the move is actualized, whether the move is communal and/or personal, whether the move is by choice or by force, and whether the new sites are locations for conformity or freedom. This examination, a new and important study of African American women's literature, also considers the final outcome of black women's movement from within, in-between, and beyond spaces of differences.

Theoretical Frame for Study

Aside from answering the aforementioned questions, this examination looks at themes of black female identity and autonomy. Because female narratives of enslavement offer a description of the oppression of black women, these historical novels provide a starting place to examine the black female self and her push toward female agency. Though there has been discussion of black women moving from places of oppression, I propose to extend the discussion of this movement within female narratives of enslavement that show black female characters figuratively and literally crossing borders of marginalization and repositioning themselves outside the boundaries that keep them restricted. In this examination, I investigate the ways in which female narratives show images of transgression, crossing boundaries—even boundaries of the self. Foregrounding the theoretical frame that I call the "Transient Woman," based on female movement, this book uses Homi K. Bhabha's concept of Third Space and Gloria Anzaldua's model of the "New Mestiza" to support my assertion that black female subjectivity and consciousness are realized by "going beyond" fixed boundaries. It is the crossing that provides African American women with locations to break away from racial, gender, and class differences that, as Bhabha says, "initiate new signs of identity" (*Location* 1). Succinctly, my intention is to theorize black women's movements to escape imprisoning spaces of exclusion and provide my reading of African American women writers whose fiction is concerned with a change to black female identity and position.

To analyze the ways African American women work toward self-definition and to recuperate their black female history from the colonizer, these theoretical examples provide the theoretical structure for this examination. Anzaldua's paradigm works for this study because, like African American women, Chicano women have been subjected to the dilemma of defining themselves outside the view of the hegemony. Bhabha's concept of Third Space begins and supports the idea of separate space for women creating new and distinct identities. In this separate space, one can begin the process of transforming and rejuvenating the female psyche. The Transient Woman—a new working model—is the rationale for black women's movement to sites outside the dominant order. The model here in this query explains African American women's undertaking to move out of and away from marginal locations.

Isolation or alienation for female consciousness and transformation is not a utopian view. Remaining in locations to resist hegemony does not change African American women's lives. To "sustain an ideology of resistance in the face of daily abuses," as Myriam Chancy points out, is ineffectual and relentless in places that oppress black women whose goal is radical change (13). Rather, resistance is best initiated and politicized in intervening sites. Patriarchal oppression, as Audre Lorde asserts, cannot be dismantled by using the same ideologies that sustain it. Thus, black female transformation must take place in sites outside the powers that view African American women as inadequate. Taking this into consideration, I conceptualize a model of the Transient Woman to show the movement of black women from unconscious objects to deliberate forces in hegemonic society.

With these theories, I endeavor to expand the discussion of female movement using the new model of the Transient Woman and illustrate how African American women writers of narratives of resistance promote, whether intentionally or not, the idea of separate and safe space for black female subjectivity. The Transient Woman provides the rationale for why and how black women move across hegemonic borders for female transformation. Black female characters in narratives of enslavement are consciously moving to other physical and psychological spaces, refusing to be subjugated, and always creating new alternatives. This movement of new consciousness is fluid[6]—constantly moving "in and out," "back and forth," and "in-between" places while proceeding toward self-knowledge. Without such a transgression or move, the black female remains fixed in the stereotypes and myths of black womanhood that have "made it difficult for her to escape" (Deborah Gray White 28). For the Transient Woman, subjectivity and autonomy can be achieved only by a rupturing of "Otherness."

My use of the Transient Woman concept affirms black female subjectivity without positioning it as the singular way to analyze subject-hood as I borrow from Mae Gwendolyn Henderson that "as gendered and racial subjects black women speak/write in multiple voices—not all simultaneously or with equal weight, but with various and changing degrees of intensity, privileging one *parole* and then another" (137, emphasis already added). I broadly define black female subjectivity as consciousness of self in relation to others having made change to opposing views and identity, "but [also] as the [conscious and deliberate] movement which enable creative, expansive self-actualization" (hooks, "Politics" 15).

This Transient Woman paradigm connects with Anzaldua's New Mestiza and Bhabha's Third Space in my readings of female narratives of enslavement. An important feature of the New Mestiza and the Transient Woman paradigms is that they seek to subvert and question those ideologies that destabilize them in their move toward autonomy. Similarly, the New Mestiza and the Transient Woman resist ideas of essentialism. However, I propose a counterpart to Anzaldua's notion by offering an African American womanist version. Different from an interpretation of the New Mestiza "envision[ing] one provisional home where she can 'stand and claim...space'" (*Borderlands* 5), the Transient Woman does not picture a particular site or space as "home." It should be understood from this assertion that it does not imply that the Transient Woman is without a "home" or that she does not value it. Home, in this case, takes on a different meaning. Bhabha asserts that "to be unhomed is not to be homeless, nor can the 'unhomely' be easily accommodated in that familiar division of social life into private and public spheres" (*Location* 9) Notions of home, then for the Transient Woman, is temporal and is used essentially for her recovery and transformation. That home is not permanent demonstrates that the Transient Woman must continually persist in moving, progressing forever, toward her own self-definition and understanding.

The works of Myriam Chancy, Barbara Christian, Patricia Hill Collins, bell hooks, and Audre Lorde provide a beginning discussion of black women locating safe spaces for black female transformation and rejuvenation. At one end of this discussion is Tate, who asserts that, "because of the restrictions placed on the black heroine's physical movement, [the black female] must conduct her quest within close boundaries often within a room [and that] it is not her physical movement that demands our attention since it is not of primary importance" (xx). Since there has been little scholarship on the theme of movement in black women's work, particularly in female narratives of enslavement, Tate's assertion is precisely where this book argues that the black female heroine's movement is not temporary, stationary, or one whereby the female remains fixed for any extended period but is rather an advancement that shows a progression toward new sites of black female awareness.

This study is structured to demonstrate African American women writers' and black women's conscious acts in refiguring black women's positions in hegemonic order by locating sites for black female consciousness and transformation. Substantiating black women's movement, chapter 1 conceptualizes the "Transient Woman" and answers how theories of the "Transient Woman," the "New Mestiza," and Homi K. Bhabha's Third Space relate to the study of female narratives of enslavement in locating physical and psychological sites for black female consciousness and personal transformation. The chapter addresses how the movement toward black female consciousness and renewal is actualized for African American women; how the concept of Third Space relates to black women crossing boundaries in their move to self-realization; what autonomy means and how it engages African American women in the nineteenth and twentieth centuries; how black female consciousness is measured for those who once had limited access to self-knowledge; how black female subjectivity can be negotiated and realized in a white patriarchal order; and what obstacles African American women must overcome to maintain their subjectivity and independence once female transformation is actualized in women-centered spaces.

To contextualize the stereotypical images placed upon black women, my analysis begins with a chapter that describes the need for black women characters to move away from ideological locations that define them pessimistically and to step outside the parameters of nineteenth-century "true womanhood." Chapter 2 examines how the notions of space and location apply to Pauline Hopkins's *Contending Forces* (1900) and shows black heroines finding new sites to redefine black women outside the "Cult of True Womanhood." The physical spaces within female locations, such as Sappho's room and the Sewing Circle, provide sites in which Sappho and others may identify black female virtues and (re)define black womanhood at the turn of the century. Although *Contending Forces*, Hopkins's first novel, is interpreted by some as a story concerning black women and middle-class values, the novel is also about the link between African American women and places of location, demonstrating how Sappho uses women-centered spaces to redefine her black female identity.

Chapter 3 focuses on Nella Larsen's *Quicksand* (1928) and Ann Petry's *The Street* (1946) as contemporary narratives of female enslavement, examining black female characters who engage in the first three stages—innocence, consciousness, and rebelliousness—of the Transient Woman. However, Larsen and Petry's black female protagonists are examples of females who, in their move to black female consciousness, are diverted and remain at the center of dominant discourse. These women do not continue the move toward black female transformation into women-centered spaces. This chapter shows the stage of "flight" as essential in the process of change and transformation for the Transient Woman.

Chapter 4 examines Paule Marshall's *Praisesong for the Widow* (1983) and looks at the ways in which "the quality of black women's lives is affected by the interrelationship of sexism[,] racism[,]" and classism and the issue of black female identity (Christian, "Trajectories" 180). The chapter shows how upward mobility and materialism create tension and the need for a black female subject to shift from Eurocentric cultural values and influences to black female values that connect with black female consciousness. This chapter identifies the community or space African American women must inhabit in order to value and identify themselves most successfully. For Avey Johnson, black female consciousness and identity are realized when she journeys outside the borders of the United States and through what Christian identifies as "myth and ritual, precipitated by the dream of [Avey's] old great-aunt, tak[ing] her back in time and space as she prepares to move forward in consciousness" ("Trajectories" 181). This chapter examines the fourth and fifth phases of the Transient Woman that demonstrate the importance of completing the stages for black female transformation. More specifically, the chapter examines the point of entering women-centered places for renewal as the last step before reentry in hegemonic society and as part of the process toward black female subjectivity.

Chapter 5 investigates Octavia Butler's *Kindred* (1979), a narrative that focuses on the psychological, physical, and emotional forces of slavery on heroine Dana, who goes back in time to save her white slave-owner grandfather and to understand herself as a black woman in twentieth-century America. The chapter considers the fifth phase, "reentry," of the Transient Woman and its significance in her changed consciousness. Butler's story portrays the violence imposed on a black woman and her fight to remain physically and spiritually intact even when history and time persist in her extinction. The novel, then, is not only about the societal conflicts of race, gender, and class but also about the literal and figurative process of saving black women's history and existence in which this female character must, by necessity, be engaged.

These works show black women repositioning themselves in locations that advance female consciousness. Movement for these black women characters also shows African American women seeking spaces that allow for female transformation and personal autonomy. The aim here is not to prove that African American women's narratives of enslavement follow any specific model, but rather to illuminate in examining the texts in this study how black women's works act in the tradition of locating places for female subjectivity. As does Christian in *Black Women Novelists* (1980), I contend that my work here is "a beginning study that...will help readers appreciate the works of brilliant writers and will alert an interested audience to the fact that there is a rich and powerful tradition" within black women's narratives of enslavement that show the recurring theme and concern for black female realization and transformation (xi).

2

BLACK FEMALE MOVEMENT:
CONCEPTUALIZING PLACES OF
CONSCIOUSNESS FOR BLACK
FEMALE SUBJECTIVITY

A boundary is not that at which something stops but, as the Greeks recognized, the boundary is that from which *something begins its presencing.*

—Marti Heidegger[1]

Black women's literary tradition therefore includes multiple ways of interpreting existence for black women in a society that defines them narrowly—if it chooses to make visible at all.

—Joyce Pettis[2]

As a radical standpoint, perspective, position, "the politics of location" necessarily calls those of us who would participate in the formation of counter-hegemonic cultural practice to identify the spaces where we begin the process of re-vision.

—bell hooks[3]

With the increased awareness of places of locations as political has come some discussion on the subject of black women in which feminists and cultural critics try to make meaning of what space and location signify for the colonized, particularly for those who have been relegated to the margins, borders, and boundaries of center discourse in subordinate positions. At one end of thought, in regards to movement, is Tate's notion that the black woman or female heroine "must conduct her quest within close boundaries" and "she remains stationary" (Tate xx). At the other end of the spectrum is my idea that any possibilities of change for black women's positions come with a complete break or move from hegemonic practices of exclusion. It is the move from the margins and boundaries, as I suggest, that provides a safe location in which to come to terms with the black female experience and to recover black female consciousness.

bell hooks's 1990 essay "Choosing the Margin" demonstrates the reality and practices of hegemony, the powers that relegate African American women to margins, that is, margins as "oppressive boundaries" set by race and gender (*Yearning* 145). Like Audre Lorde and Myriam Chancy, who view women-centered spaces as necessary for spiritual and physical survival, hooks also sees the need to create locations that allow for black female development, creativity, and livelihood. hooks, however, unlike Lorde and Chancy, questions black women's positioning and the jeopardy into which black women are placed when they move from the margins to the center. From her view, she believes that if and when black women move from the margins, they, in essence, have to "confront the realities of choice and location" (*Yearning* 145) and decide, when considering power relations, which side offers potential for change. hooks asks the following of black women who are challenging patriarchal oppositions:

> Do we position ourselves on the side of colonizing mentality? Or do we continue to stand in resistance with the oppressed…ready to offer our ways of seeing and theorizing…towards that revolutionary effort which seeks to create space…where transformation is possible? (*Yearning* 145)

According to hooks, such questions call for considering the places where there are possibilities for African American women to realize and articulate oppositional acts for change. The radical place for resistance, as hooks profoundly believes, is on the margins—"a profound edge" (149). Inasmuch as hooks believes change and resistance can be realized on and from the borders, hooks's essay and these questions spawn an examination of African American women's position where their "difference" unquestionably means a place on the margins of white dominant society. In hegemonic order, race and gender identify those who have power and those who do not. Thus, power in this sense is about articulating one's existence and exercising autonomy. To do this means, particularly for African American women, to understand one's place in the social order (Tate 55), which ultimately enables their own self-agency and self-determination.

In examining the use of space in African American women's self-realization, I argue that the choice for black female transformation comes with the knowledge of one's position in a white male–dominated, racist/classist society and of a black woman's choice to move from locations that distort, disrupt, and disengage her very existence. To remain in these former sites is to bring self-destruction, since these locations cannot provide possibilities for personal change and female subjectivity. In fact, early African American women's writings show the disastrous consequences women experience in being isolated within and who remain in that "other" space. These works portray as well the direct affect on the psyche of women who do not return to black female–centered spaces for female renewal. Helga Crane in Nella Larsen's *Quicksand* (1928) and Lutie Johnson in Ann Petry's *The Street* (1946) are examples of strong black women who lose themselves while trying to realize black female identity in the wrong places. Helga comes close to connecting with herself after she refuses to marry a white suitor who sees her as an object to possess. Yet she is in the same position as possession when she accepts the Reverend Pleasant Green's proposal. Helga finds nothing "pleasant" about her life as a minister's wife or as a mother of five. In fact, she is shattered and destroyed by both of these identities. Lutie Johnson's destruction comes in her delusions about the American Dream. Living and working for a white middle-class family, Lutie absorbs the notion that she can live the American way of life by having the ideal marriage, living within a secure environment, and providing adequate schooling for her son Bub. Lutie is destroyed by an American Dream that excludes black women. Because of their misconceptions about black women's place in white society and the misrepresentation of material goods, Helga's and Lutie's lives come to disastrous ends.

Through the lens of both novels, we see direct correlation to the consequences for African American women who remain in places that dehumanize and prevent self-realization. Both Helga and Lutie show that existing on the borders of hegemonic society creates for them disillusionment and disappointment. For Helga, ideas of moving away from black stereotypes in America are reinforced only in Denmark. Respectability and self-reliance as a black woman are no longer expressed when she is viewed as an "exotic peacock" and an object of possession for the highest "bidder" with the best social standings. Lutie's happiness is never realized on 116th Street despite her efforts of trying to provide a better life for herself and her son Bub. Lutie's belief in the American Dream is shattered when she is not taken seriously in her pursuing a position as a stenographer and singer. Instead she is viewed by men and women as a sexual object; her female sexuality is a liability in a place where women are seen implicitly as sexual beings. Thus, hooks's argument for using the margins as a place of resistance, particularly for African American women, does not provide possibilities for change or for the prospect to be viewed differently.

The argument here for radical change in places beyond borders and boundaries is neither pessimistic nor disillusioned, as in hooks's sense of situating the disenfranchised on the margins. My argument points out that for African American women to change their peripheral position in white society, they must move from the margins fixed by hegemony to sites that allow them to create new identities as whole and informed women. Though hooks's argument and the case here are different in contending the ideal place for repositioning black women, both claims are alike in pointing to and using the same justification for locating safe places for black women's survival and change. However, the idea of safe space for transformation is a critical concept for refiguring black women's subjectivity, particularly since African Americans have always been the "watched" and the "watchee" from places on the margins. Lorde asserts, "In order to survive those of us for whom oppression is as American as apple pie have always had to be watchers." Significantly, "this 'watching' generates a dual consciousness in African-American women, one in which black women 'become familiar with the language and manners of the oppressor, even sometimes adopting them for some illusion of protection'" (Collins 97).

With a detailed description of the stereotypes and myths that serve to marginalize African American women, this chapter shows the causes and effects of cultural suppression that propel black women to locate new sites for black female subjectivity. The next part of this discussion shows how black women in general and black women writers in particular focus on changing these images of African American women. Another section argues the critical need and significance of locating black female–centered spaces. Because this study centers on movement and places for self-sufficiency, the chapter claims that African American women's narratives of enslavement demonstrate black women's concern for finding new sites for self-definition. Following a discussion, the study considers and describes how female movement, through the concept of the Transient Woman, is realized. It also explains and describes the progression in stages of the Transient Woman. An important part of looking at the five stages in black female development is considering Bhabha's concept of Third Space relative to black female consciousness and subjectivity. The final part of this argument explains the consequences for black women, who, after progressing from Third Space and "Beyond" and emerging into locations of dominant discourse, do not return to black female–centered locations for renewal.

Myths of African American Women

Part of the negative images of African American women is portrayed in contemporary society as "mammy," "jezebel," and sapphire have their roots in slavery. Such imagery, as projected in the eighteenth and nineteenth centuries, follows from the myths and stereotypes that whites associated with African American women as being depraved and promiscuous. Other depictions characterized them, including black men, as "infantile, irresponsible, submissive, and promiscuous" ("The Jezebel and Mammy" 27). The last description has been one of the most difficult to dispel because of the imagery of black women as loose and immoral. Whether as the most prevailing image or not, the notion of African American women as licentious is just as damaging as the portrayal of the mammy figure "in maintaining oppressions of gender and sexuality" (Collins 73). Basically, the point about derogatory and stereotypical images of African American women is that holders of power use these for the purpose of maintaining power in hegemony society.

The mammy representation not only comes from the view of black women acting as caretaker and nurturer of the white family but it also serves to "symbolize the dominant groups' perceptions of the ideal Black female relationship to elite White male power"[4] as faithful and obedient servant. Some of these depictions are derived from "memoirs written after the Civil War" (White 47). "According to these accounts, Mammy was the woman who could do anything…Because of her expertise in all domestic matters, she was the premier house servant" (47). Considering the mammy image as the Other, she was portrayed as overweight, overbearing, sexless, and manly. As hooks asserts, whites depicted the black female as masculine because "they saw her ability to endure hardships no 'lady' was supposedly capable of enduring" (hooks, *Ain't* 82). Her value lay in her uncomplaining toughness and ability to care for whites and their families while at the same time having to neglect her own immediate family. "She was, in short," as White claims, "surrogate mistress and mother" (49).

As exemplified in the film *Gone with the Wind* (1939), Hattie McDaniel plays the boisterous mammy to the O'Hara's family. She is domineering and often unruly. Viewed as nonthreatening to the family, Mammy takes liberties in talking back and ordering white family members; she tells Scarlet when to eat, when to sleep, and how a "lady" should act. Whereas a female slave working in the fields would have been easily whipped and/or even sold from the plantation for her behavior, Mammy is not. Mammy in *Gone with the Wind* is depicted unrealistically compared to the realities for a female house slave. However, the movie does provide a faithful portrayal of the mammy character in relation with her own family. The audience never sees Mammy talking and interacting with her own family, or even with other blacks outside the white O'Hara household.

Marlon T. Riggs's film *Ethnic Notions* (1987) provides another vivid depiction of the mammy figure and how the stereotype that originated in slavery remains in the minds of society even today. One such example used in the film shows the mammy wildly excited about the young white master having returned home from a trip to the north. Dropping everything, which included caring for her own family, Mammy exudes unquenchable excitement in preparing a large feast for the returning master. The mammy's purpose, whites believed, was to serve the white family, placing them at the center of her concern even above her own family. As is demonstrated in *Gone with the Wind* (1939) and critiqued in *Ethnic Notions,* the mammy figure is an image of a black woman who is a long-suffering maternal figure whose greatest value is her unconditional love and loyalty for the white family she serves faithfully and willingly.[5] Besides portraying the mammy as self-sacrificing and willing to please, negative representations have suggested that the mammy figure is sexless, thus making her seemingly undesirable to white males and no threat to white wives.

The mammy is also created in her character as a nonsexual being. Though white males did have relations with their slave women, the stereotype of the sexless mammy helped allay fears that white wives had of white men forming liaisons with young black women. As mentioned, the mammy is typically depicted as obese and as exerting masculine strength; she is also viewed as unclean, in her greasy dirty head rag, and has large feet that further show masculine and animalistic features. Because of her stereotypical characteristics, white men feigned public disinterest in the sexuality of African American women. For example, because of Sojourner Truth's large stature, audiences sometimes alluded to her as a man in disguise. On one speaking circuit, Truth was challenged to prove she was a woman. By baring her breast, she chastised the young male by saying that she had nursed many a white baby at her breast. Defiantly, Truth exposed her breast to show she was a woman in every way (Truth 95). The idea that Truth breastfeeds is indication that she had been sexually active and had had a baby and thus proves Truth, like other black women/mothers, to be desirable.

The notion of the sexless, undesirable mammy is contradicted by whites' stereotype of African American women as promiscuous. In direct contrast to white mistresses in the antebellum South, African American women were seen as the opposite of the pure, chaste, and moral white female icons of "true womanhood." While they were not viewed as humans or women, young black women were often deemed by the American public as "sexually permissive, as available and eager for the sexual assaults of any man, black or white" (hooks, *Ain't* 52). As previously noted, the image of black women being oversexed and sexually willing has its beginnings in slavery. Because of their positions as slaves and without black male protection, female slaves were often used for the sexual pleasure of white slave owners. Antebellum female slave narratives describe the sexual advances black women experienced from their white slave masters. Without explicit details of sexual acts, most female slave narrators tell only of the advances and threats made upon them to cooperate in sexual acts. Presumably African American women would not want to disclose sexual graphic details in order to not perpetuate existing myths about their sexual being. Rather they would most likely prefer for their audience to focus on the violence of slavery and inflame the desire to abolish it.

While slave narratives were used by former slaves and abolitionists to expose human abuse, female slave narratives did provide enough details to confirm sexual abuse without feeding into white's desire for sexual sensationalism. In her amanuensis's curiosity about the sexual act between herself and her slave owner, the interviewer's questions center on what followed the assault and asks Louisa Picquet "What happened next?" (*Collected Women's Narratives, Louisa Picquet, The Octoroon*, 11). Aware of her amanuensis's heightened interest in the sexual activities between master and slave, Picquet purposely fills in her story with long unimportant details. It is apparent to Picquet that the male interviewer is more interested in the sexual act than the abuse when he asks, "How were you dressed—with thin clothes, or how?" (12). In futile efforts to claim the same conditions as virtuous white women's, Picquet presents herself as an unwilling partner in sex outside marriage. Picquet purposely distances herself from any sexual connotations in answering that

"In the summertime we never wore but two pieces" (12). Here Picquet cleverly moves the attention from herself and places it on the community of slaves and the lightly veiled clothes they wore in the summer.[6]

Warding off the white master's intent of rape was not always successful for some female slaves. Harriet Jacobs in *Incidents in the Life of a Slave Girl* portrays her sexual history by craftily appealing to her white audience's pity and asking them not to judge her harshly for her sexual activity during her enslavement. In her attempt to ward off stereotypes about black female promiscuity, Jacobs asks that her white female audience understand the situation of female slaves in the South and not hold them to the same standards as white middle-class women. Linda (Jacobs's pseudonym) appeals to her readers:

> Pity me, and pardon me, O virtuous reader! You never knew what it is to be a slave; to be entirely unprotected by law or custom; to the have the laws reduce you to the condition of a chattel, entirely subject to the will of another.... Still, in looking back, calmly, on the events of my life, I feel that the slave woman ought not to be judged by the same standard as others. (56)

As a female slave, Linda/Harriet does more than struggle with slavery; she fights to gain freedom of her body, her memory, and herself. What is particularly revealing here, too, is Jacobs' efforts in adhering to the tenets of True Womanhood. The character Linda Brent had learned earlier from her grandmother about appropriate female behavior in matters of sex before marriage. Linda's grandmother is devastated upon learning her sexual transgression and exclaims: "O Linda! has it come to this? I had rather see you dead than to see you as you are. You are a disgrace to your dead mother" (56). The grandmother's reaction to Linda's wrongdoing demonstrates that African American women maintained the same values for a virtuous woman as their white counterparts. Marli F. Weiner, in "Slave Women Confront the Ideology of Domesticity," writes, "Like whites, blacks developed a set of expectations defining appropriate behavior for men and women. Those expectations blended African practices, and, by the antebellum years, centuries of

African American cultural development" (113). Regardless of slavery, African Americans upheld their African values and societal standards on good decorum for a nineteenth-century woman.

Despite the black woman's attempts over time to uphold the virtues of true womanhood, it has not been easy for her to escape the many myths surrounding her sexuality. In antebellum America, African American women earned the label of jezebel, depicted as loose, oversexed, and willing partners in sex relations with men.[7] The jezebel image, White notes, is "fully as misleading" as the mammy figure (49). In one sense, the black woman is viewed as a nonsexual object; in another, she is "a person governed almost entirely by her libido" (White 29). By nineteenth-century hegemony standards, the black woman was everything but the ideal of the Victorian female (29). She was not considered or deemed pious, virtuous, or domestic. Because of her allegedly forceful sexual nature and from whites' initial impressions, the black woman was considered a viable target for sexual abuse. In fact, these misconceptions then provided a rationale for white male sexual assaults on black enslaved women. Sexualized reports from sixteenth-century abolitionist William Smith fueled the myths about the black woman's sexuality. In *A New Voyage to Guinea,* Smith portrays black women as "hot constitution'd Ladies" who "are continually contriving strategems how to gain a lover" and that primates "often attack and use Violence to the Black Women whenever they meet them alone in the Woods" (Quoted by White 29). Such biased and racialized reports only inflamed notions of exaggeratedly sexed black women.

Following Reconstruction, myths about African American women continued to politicize racial discourses on black womanhood. When black women might have exerted greater control over their minds and bodies, black women were stereotyped as Sapphires. As the counterpart to the mammy image, the Sapphire image depicted black women as "evil, treacherous, bitch, stubborn, and hateful, in short all that the mammy figure was not" (hooks, *Ain't* 85). Most damaging in the use of the Sapphire image is black women typecasted as emasculating black men. Unfortunately this stereotype prevails and was particularly damaging at the beginning of the surge of black women writers in the 1980s. The success of Alice Walker's *The Color Purple* (1982) was tainted by critics who accused her as the embodiment of the black women's literary movement characterized by black male bashing. Likewise, Ntozake Shange's *For Colored Girls Who Have Considered Suicide* (1975) had been earlier accused of presenting negative representations of black men. The crux of it all points to the perpetuation of stereotypes that debase African American women. While such stereotypes about black women are racially and sexually charged, they unfortunately continue to provide the "master" with tools for placing African American women on the margin.

Another biased stereotype that has come to prevail through today is the idea of the strong black woman. Because hegemonic ideologies offer African American women as resilient and able to endure hardships, as in the stereotype of the mammy figure, some black women have internalized the notion that they are to tolerate and "put up" with being victims. Patricia Hill Collins points out, "abused women, particularly those bearing the invisible scars of emotional abuse, are often silenced by the image of the 'superstrong' Black woman" (159). Some young black girls have witnessed their emotionally and physically abused mothers keeping silent and accepted their mother's response as what strong black women do to keep their families in tact. An example of female abuse and a woman trying to break her silence is found in Zora Neale Hurston's *Their Eyes Were Watching God* (1937). Janie, in response to her husband, Jody, comparing women to animals, tries to hint at his abusive nature. Jody, in the presence of other men, responds by criticizing Janie's intelligence; the response causes added damage to Janie's self-esteem:

> *Jody*: "Somebody got to think for women and chillum and chickens and cows. I god, they sho don't think none their selves."
> *Janie*: "Ah knows uh few things, and womenfolks thinks sometimes too!"
> *Jody*: "Aw naw they don't. They just think they's thinkin'. When ah see one thing Ah understands ten. You see ten things and don't understand one." (Hurston 66–67)

Although Janie knows that most of the men recognize that Jody is responding this way because she tries to fight back, she is hurt and turns inwardly. There were times before when she "fought back with her tongue." Janie understands that Jody, as the big man in town, "want[s] her submission and he'd keep on fighting until he felt he had it." So instead she would act upon the idea of the strong black woman and "press her teeth together and learn to hush" (67). Unfortunately, the advice given by Nanny to "better leave things de way dey is…Yo mind will change" works and moves Janie to silence and putting up with Jody's psychological abuse. "Unfortunately, Nanny's lessons," as DoVeanna Fulton asserts, "are born of pragmatism based on lived experience circumscribed by the institution of slavery that does not include a mutually satisfying heterosexual relationship" (83). The remnants of slavery carried over the idea that survival depended on women being silent and "putting up with" abuse from the "master."

In a later relationship, Janie's new beau, Tea Cake, does not prove to be "a bee for her bloom" (101). In his idea to work against the threat of Mrs. Turner's light-skinned brother, Tea Cake attempts to show Mrs. Turner and the men in the Everglades that Janie belongs to him: "Before the week was over he had whipped Janie. Not because her behavior justified his jealousy, but it relieved that awful fear inside him. Being able to whip her reassured him in possession" (140).[8] Though it is the abuser who has a low self-esteem in exerting power over others, emotionally abused women sometimes act powerless to appear submissive, which shows she accepts her role as the lesser one in the relationship. However, this does not always prove the case for Janie when she later fights back. Accepting the role of the submissive woman as a sign of a "good" or "true" woman, black women also buy into hegemonic practices in their marriages. Such examples as the one here show how African American women believe and have unconsciously accepted the roles assigned to them as "strong women" and are less inclined to call for help, believing they can "handle it on [their] own" (as quoted by Collins 159).

Conversely, some African American women reject all these images and yet fall into another stereotype, that of the materialistic woman. By seeking men with wealth and class status, they reinscribe the contemporary controlling image of some women as being materialistic and focused only on wealth and class. In her article "Sensuous Sapphires: A Study of the Social Construction of Black Female Sexuality," Annecka Marshall discusses "how black women perceive the controlling images applied to them and how they negotiated those images in shaping their sexual [and social] selves" (qtd. in Collins 156). Instead of black women, as in the previous examples, seeing that it devaluates the idea of black womanhood, they continue the white prevailing script of oppressed black femininity and sexual politics.

This idea of marrying for social class and money is observed with characters Clare Kendry and Irene Redfield in Nella Larsen's *Passing* (1929). Clare sacrifices her black identity when she marries a white male whom she believes offers her more prospects for economic security and status. However, her security, martially and economically, is falsely based on her passing as a white female married to a white spouse. When Clare asks Irene why she has not thought of passing, Irene answers that there is no reason for her to pass when she is content with what she has " 'except, perhaps, a little more money' " (Larsen 160). This is not entirely true, for Irene passes when it is for her personal convenience. Clare reinforces the negative image of the "kept woman" in her superior answer to Irene:

> " 'Of course…that's what everybody wants, just a little more money, even the people who have it. And I must say I don't blame them. Money's awfully nice to have. In fact, all things considered, I think, 'Rene, that it's even worth the price.' " (Larsen 160)

Clare's views emphasize the idea that women can and do place themselves in the male marketplace by surrendering their female "erotic"[9] and identity to a predominant focus on materiality.

Like Larsen, Hurston in "The Gilded Six-Bits" (1933) examines the constraints placed by materiality on the female erotic in the context of marriage. Hurston's work thematically shows the character Missie May defeated both by her lack of female knowledge and by her misuse of female sexuality. From my revisionist's reading of the short story, I argue that Hurston's female character functions as wife and sexual property in sexual games, as commodity in a male exchange, and as mother/wife who gains added value only when she produces a male heir[10] (Myles). Essentially, Missie May, in the act of misappropriating her female "erotic," becomes merely desirable property for the desires of men. Fulton comments that "these love relationships coupled with domestic violence...are a consequence of the society's inclination to view women as possessions and objects" (89).[11] Domestic violence, in the case of Missie May, is her husband's exploiting her body and psyche in exchange for marital security.

Male exploitation of African American women's sexuality and female body takes the same form as the slave auction block. In some cases during slavery, as Collins points out, "the entire body itself became commodified" (132). Slave bidders were interested in the black female womb in speculating profits from breeding her with the slave master's plantation "buck." In essence, the slave master tries to have complete control over the black female body—her womb and vagina. In *The History of Mary Prince* (1831), Prince describes the pain and horror she and her sisters experienced:

> We followed my mother to the market-place, where she placed us in a row against a large house, with our backs to the wall and arms folded across our breasts....At length the vendue master, who was to offer us for sale like sheep or cattle arrived....He...[,] turning me slowly around, exposed me to the view of those who attended the vendue. I was soon surrounded by strange men, who examined and handled me in the same manner that a butcher would a calf or a lamb he was about to purchase. (4)

Prince vividly reconstructs the pain and exploitation she feels in the gaze and hands of white male strangers. No longer in control of her body, Prince is reduced to an animal and can only look on as she is awarded to the highest bidder.

The figurative and literal rape of black women's identities, through the racialized, sexualized, and politicized stereotypes, is a result of the continual devaluation of black women and hegemonic oppressive practices. As mentioned earlier, this devaluation, in part, comes out past white male practices in removing "woman" from the definition of black womanhood in order to make her an object and slave. Unfortunately, this process did not stop even after the end of slavery. Racist and sexist societal views of black women subsist even now while African American women seek to challenge and change how others view them as women. Because self-defining is critical for black female subjectivity, African American women must continue to be at the forefront in their movement toward a new identity and place in society. This process includes not only African America women recognizing what has been said about them, but that they must also question the intentions of those possessing the power to define (114). Nikki Giovanni makes clear these connections among self, change, and self-empowerment: "We got to live in the real world. If we don't' like the world we're living in, change it. And if we can't change it, we change ourself. We can do something" (as quoted by Collins 117). When black women persist in defining themselves, the "act of insisting on black female self-definition [will] validate black women's power as human subjects" and authority as transformed African American women (Collins 114).

THE TASK OF CHANGING BLACK WOMEN'S IMAGE

The mission to change negative images of black womanhood has been at the forefront of black women's quest for self-definition. As early as slavery, African American women have worked tirelessly to alter white patriarchy's definition of black womanhood. Such an example is found in Maria W. Stewart's first published essay "Religion and the Pure Principles of Morality, The Sure Foundation on Which We Must Build" (1831). Though her essay is addressed to all African Americans, the following passage points to Stewart's efforts in rallying black women to laboriously work toward changing how they are viewed by others. She writes,

> I am of a strong opinion that the day on which we unite, heart and soul, and turn our attention to knowledge and improvement, that day the hissing and reproach among the nations of the earth against us will cease. And even those who now point at us with the finger of scorn, will aid and befriend us. It is of

no use for us to sit with our hands folded, hanging our heads like bulrushes, lamenting our wretched condition; but let us make a mighty effort, and arise; and if none will promote or respect us, let us promote and respect ourselves. (Richardson 37)

While Stewart acknowledges that others might be slow in acknowledging a change in their conditions, she believes it is better to make the effort than wait for others to do it for them. The possibility of changing the stereotypes and views of others, according to Stewart, can transpire through group persistence and a changed consciousness.

In *Incidents in the Life of a Slave Girl*, Jacobs provides another example of an early African American woman who understands that change does come with some risk and group effort. She compromises her womanhood and courageously exposes her sexual history to reveal the real culprit in debasing black women's femininity and sexuality. In her narrative, she admits her iniquity: "I know I did wrong. No one can feel it more sensibly than I do" (55). However, she defends her action by sharing that she was flattered by the attention of a single white gentleman for a slave girl. In her quest to expose the conditions of slavery for black women and to defend black womanhood, Jacobs, as Linda Brent, appeals to a white female audience to understand her motives as a willing sexual partner with a white male:

> I wanted to keep myself pure; and, under the most adverse circumstances, I tried hard to preserve my self-respect; but I was struggling alone in the powerful grasp of the demon Slavery; and the monster proved too strong for me. I felt as if I was forsaken by God and man; as if all my efforts must be frustrated; and I became reckless in my despair. (54)

After detailing the constant conditions in which a young female slave lives, Jacobs defends herself by showing the naivety of a poor slave girl of fifteen who is flattered by being given "so much attention from a superior person" (54). She rationalizes her actions as natural feelings of any young girl:

> It seems less degrading to give one's self, than to submit to compulsion. There is something akin to freedom in having a lover

> who has no control over you, except that which he gains by kind-
> ness and attachment.... There may be sophistry in all this; but
> the condition of a slave confuses all principles of morality, and,
> in fact, renders the practice of them impossible. (Jacobs 55)

Jacobs takes responsibility for her choices but delicately shows that like any young female, she felt and acted recklessly upon her feelings. By characterizing herself as vulnerable, Jacobs positions herself with white women and shows she is no different from them and should not be deemed as licentious.

From the ongoing mythologizing of African American women, black women, critics, and scholars understand that their efforts have to be ongoing and persistent to "cut through layers of institutionalized racism and sexism" (Tate xvi). By some indications, black women's task of changing the controlling images of African American women has not been simple.[12] In confronting these negative images, black women face and experience sexist and racist labels for speaking out. As Cheryl Gilkes contends,

> Black women's assertiveness and their use of every expression of racism to launch multiple assaults against the entire fabric of inequality have been a consistent, multifaceted threat to the status quo. As punishment, black women have been assaulted with a variety of negative images. ("From Slavery to Social Welfare" 294)

What are the reasons for hegemony practices in reproving black women who speak out against the persistent detrimental images of themselves? How might African American women alter these false notions when the "powers that be" define societal values and thus manipulate the ideas about black women and their social position?

To remove the constraints of black female oppression and move from the margin, African American women must define themselves in their own words and by their own ideologies of black female identity. As one of the most devalued female groups in hegemonic society, African American women have suffered from both male and white female abuse. In *A Voice from the South* (1892), Anna Julia Cooper makes this point when describing incidents of deliberate abuse of black women traveling by public transportation: train conductors "handing woman after woman from the steps to the stool…or else relieving her of satchels and bags and enabling her to make the descent easily, deliberately fold their arms and turn around when the Black Woman's turn came to alight" (90). Having been constantly ignored and disrespected, she endures but carries the pain of black womanhood. Cooper describes the emotion: "The feeling of slighted womanhood is unlike every other emotion of the soul" (90). And when the disrespect comes from those who are trained in courtesy, Cooper asserts, the censure of a man regarding a female's womanhood is amplified. Likewise, when other women devalue and exploit black women's existence, the condemnation is intensified. In "An Open Letter to Mary Daly," Lorde admonishes Daly for implying that all women, both black and white, suffer the same kinds of male oppression (67). Lorde alleges, "I am used to having my archetypal experience distorted and trivialized, but it is terribly painful to feel it being done by a woman whose knowledge so much touches my own" (68).

Because only the black woman feels and knows the pain from the devaluation of her black womanhood, it is she who can and must articulate the possibilities for change. In the case of African American women, the idea that the victim is in the best position to speak for his or her own change is enhanced by Tawawa Chimney Corner, who writes, "As our Caucasian barristers are not to blame if they cannot *quite* put themselves in the dark man's place, neither should the dark man be wholly expected fully and adequately to reproduce the exact Voice of the Black Woman" (Cooper, *A Voice* III). The work to change visions of African American women is a task for black women.[13]

Inasmuch as African American women and white women experience sexism from disparate positions of power, their concerns are unlike when speaking and writing about African American women's lived experiences. Indirectly, this is the point that Christian expresses in her essay "The Race for Theory" concerning white feminists and others whose discourse places black women at a disadvantage. Christian writes,

> I could go on critiquing the positions of French feminists who are themselves more various in their points of view than

the label which is used to describe them. . . . What I am concerned about is the authority this school now has in feminist scholarship—the way it has become *authoritative discourse,* monologic, which occurs precisely because it does have access to the means of promulgating its ideas. ("Race" 356)

The apprehension on Christian's part follows from what she sees as white feminists becoming the unquestioned authority in all aspects of women's experience. Basically, Christian's argument points to the importance of African American women defining black womanhood outside others' notions of womanhood. White feminists, as Christian asserts, made a place for themselves in theoretical discourse, so too must African American women assert their authority in speaking to issues of black women's experience and black feminist ideology. Lorde explains why black women are compelled to define themselves. She writes, "For Black women . . . it is axiomatic that if we do not define ourselves for ourselves, we will be defined by others—for their use and to our detriment" (45). From Lorde's view, it is imperative that African American women position themselves so that a definition about black womanhood is one that is constructed from their own lived experiences and oppressions.

Black Female Movement toward a New Black Female Consciousness

In the move to change how black women are defined, a changed consciousness is necessary. Any meaningful change or the desire to alter what is the current status requires a rupture, or a revolutionary change from the status quo. In a revolution, whether literal or figurative, there is an overthrow of the ideology that places the subject in its oppressive condition. The change comes not from the oppressor but from the oppressed. Toni Cade Bambara writes, "Revolution begins with the self, in the self. The individual, the basic revolutionary unit, must be purged of poison and lies that assault the ego and threaten the heart" (109).[14] For a radical cleansing of ideas that disrupt female wholeness, reform and recovery must begin with a transformation from within.

Female slave narratives and black women's literature reveal the basis of a changed consciousness and the authority of black women to move from the negative images placed upon them. Described by others as unlearned, Truth, in the *Narrative of Sojourner Truth*, demonstrates how she uses her illiteracy to change the views of white educated audiences. That others "listened eagerly to Truth, and . . . whole audience melted into tears by her touching stories" (*Narrative* 77) demonstrates her rhetorical skills in public speaking. Fulton credits Truth's rhetorical abilities to the oral traditions of African American communities. Asserting that Truth's skills are demonstrated not so much from what scholars have long recognized as skills learned from "her antislavery and women's rights speeches," Fulton claims that Truth's speaking skills "demonstrates the foundation of the oral discursive strategies she learned as a child from her parents that she later employed in public speaking" (26). Elizabeth Keckley in *Behind the Scenes* describes in her Post-Reconstruction slave narrative how she moves away from the mindset that she "would never be worth her salt" (91). With a changed consciousness in realizing her value as a person, Keckley redefines herself as a free woman and later as an accomplished modiste to Mrs. Abraham Lincoln. Janette Alston, in Frances Ellen Watkins Harper's "The Two Offers" (1859), alters the social idea that happiness for women is realized only through marriage when she shows that self-fulfillment can be achieved as a single woman. In Zora Neale Hurston's *Their Eyes Were Watching God* (1937), Janie Crawford combats suppressing her female identity and sexuality and finds the "dust-bearing bee" with Tea Cake on her own terms. The women in Ntozake Shange's *For Colored Girls* (1974) change their altered states of "havin been a girl['s] half-notes scattered without rhythm" to becoming women with a new song "repeat[ing] . . . the lines 'i found god in myself & loved her'" (63). Black women's writings as the ones here affirm the importance of a changed consciousness and that African American women from all classes and times opposed positions as the Other.

As Collins points out, "Resisting by doing something that 'is not expected' could not have occurred without Black women's long-standing rejection of mammies, matriarchs, and other controlling images" (98). In essence, there is among black women a "distinctive, collective Black women's consciousness" (98). Black women's acts of defiance in "talking back" to the oppressor, spoken or unspoken, are the basis of African American women's survival. Although resistance is the active force to begin any change, the act of opposition is not necessarily enough for a radical change (hooks, *Yearning* 15). Coupled with black women's defiance is the necessity of moving out from oppressive sites to women-centered spaces that allow for female renewal. Opposition, as acted out in the heat of the moment, is short-lived (hooks 15). Thus, resistance to hegemony ideology must be a continual long-term process. The process, in this study, is one that sustains and affirms black female subjectivity while securing freedom from fixed marginalized places.

The movement to black female subjectivity, as envisioned here, materializes with deliberate awareness and effort. As such, a purposeful consciousness comes from an understanding of what holds one from the possibility of personal autonomy. Knowledge means power and is critical for African American women in understanding the inner power that Lorde describes. In "Uses of the Erotic," Lorde writes, "Recognizing the power of the erotic within our lives can give us the energy to pursue genuine change within our world, rather than merely settling for a shift of character in the same weary drama" (59). The power to which Lorde refers is one that all women possess—what she identifies as the "erotic." Unlike the patriarchal definition of erotic as sexual, Lorde's erotic is characterized by the acceptance and a change of the female self. This appreciation and movement of the psyche is dynamic because it allows the female to demand more of herself and instructs not to readily accept substandard behavior from others. Lorde explains that when women become empowered by their "erotic" knowledge, they are able to inspect the variables in their lives and provide the efficacy to change their existence in the places that oppress them. Lorde writes,

> This is one reason why the erotic is so feared...[by patriarchy]. For once we begin to feel deeply all the aspects of our lives, we begin to demand from ourselves and from our life-pursuits that

they feel in accordance with that joy which we know ourselves to be capable of. Our erotic knowledge empowers us, becomes a lens through which we scrutinize all aspects of our existence, forcing us to evaluate those aspects honestly in terms of their relative meaning within our lives. And this is a grave responsibility, projected from within each of us, not to settle for the convenient, the shoddy, the conventionally expected, nor the merely safe. (57)

Once African American women are aware of the power they have to change, it is their moral obligation to themselves to move away from sites that continue to devalue them as women.

Even the minor character Min in Petry's *The Street* uses her inner female power and moves out of her oppressive state with the satanic "Supe" Jones. Min finds her strength in knowing that she does not have to accept the habitual abuse from Jones. Having once accepted the idea that "a woman by herself didn't stand much chance; and because it was too lonely living by herself" (133), Earlier Min had misinterpreted the idea that it is safer to stay in places of abuse than leaving them. Min thought that "with a man attached to her she could have an apartment—a real home" even at the risk of losing her life physically and spiritually (133). Her moment of moving away from her oppressive state and relationship with Jones comes when she *deliberately* plans her escape after a verbal altercation with him. In this moment, Min takes responsibility for her existence and consciously uses her "erotic" power and "give[s] up, of necessity, being satisfied with suffering and self-negation" with Satanic Supe Jones (Lorde 58). Min's act against her oppressor and oppression becomes, as Lorde describes, "integral with self, motivated and empowered from within" (58). Moving away from places that oppress and subjugate women must be calculated and swift.

The shift or movement from sites of oppression to other settings reveals black women's progression toward black female consciousness. The model that illustrates movement or change, in this study, uses a postcolonial paradigm that shows African American women being situated at the edge of white social order. White social order positions black women on the border to continue black women's subjugation that keeps them intact in white male-dominated society. At the same time, such social positioning maintains a divisive line between white feminists and African American women, which in turn further restricts black women to subordinate positions under white females. The movements that show black women shifting from places of oppression occur from "margin to center," "outside to inside," and "inside to outside" and portray their existence as "in-between" or cross-"borders/boundaries," or in some cases at the "center." The subversion of Otherness is realized when black women move from positions of marginality to create a dialogue with the "center." The processes in which they "talk back" to the center include the denial of center to exercise authority over black female definition and the rejection of past definitions and labels used by hegemony.[15] The second part of the progression follows with a break from the "center" and its surrounding or enclosed space. The ongoing process toward black female consciousness, through the Transient Woman's concept, completes the break when black women move to Third Space to formulate new self-meaning as self-defined subjects.

MODELS FOR BLACK FEMALE MOVEMENT

The Transient Woman[16]

The idea of the "Transient Woman," as I conceptualize it, makes clearer the process in which African American women move to black female consciousness and female subjectivity. "Transient" movements are psychological, spiritual, and political. Psychologically, the movement points to the process of black women changing how they view themselves. No longer willing to remain on the margins, African American women move away from places that disrupt their own ideas and visions for themselves. Spiritually, black women shift from locations they once retreated into—insanity—to sites that allow both growth and development. African American women gather personal resources through a spiritual connection with women like themselves. Politically, movement is against oppression, and black women confront and contest hegemonic forces. Coming from the edge of indifference, these women move into and from regions that once denied their existence. Lorde provides the language to express this "revolutionary demand." She asserts that "the white fathers told us: I think, therefore I am. The Black mother within each of us—the poet—whispers in our dreams: I feel, therefore I can be free" (38). The Transient Woman, using the historical violation of African American women, conceptually works to show how black women revise and recreate new identities in their move toward black female subjectivity.

In this study, I argue that the process toward the Transient Woman is realized through five stages: Innocence, Consciousness, Rebelliousness, Flight (Digression), and Reentry (Materialization). The Transient Woman's initial "Innocence" stage relates to female existence within an idyllic environment. Her immediate surroundings center in or near family or a community support system. Like Janie Crawford in Hurston's *Their Eyes Were Watching God*, there is a sweet and pure innocence about the female character who exists in a moment not yet exposed to the "place" of difference and Other. Deborah Gray White's assertion that "slave girls childhood was neither carefree nor burdensome" (92) is countered by the testimonies of past female slaves. Former slave Lucy Delaney expresses in her narrative, "How well [she] remembered those happy days! Slavery had no horror for [her], as [she] played about the place, with the same joyful freedom as the little white children." She remembers, "With mother, father, and sister, a pleasant home surroundings, what happier child than I!" (Delaney, *Six Women's Narratives* 13). Harriet Jacobs in her narrative claims that she "was born a slave; but…never knew it till six years of happy childhood had passed away" and that she "was so fondly shield that [she] never dreamed [she] was a piece of merchandise" (Jacobs 5). Kate Drumgoold in *A Slave Girl's Story* (1897) expresses in her life story that she "was feeling as free [as] anyone could feel" when she was a girl in Old Virginia. Similarly, the innocent granddaughter of the servant Nanny, Janie Crawford, in Hurston's *Their Eyes Were Watching God*, does not recognize that she is black until she is pointed out in a photo: " 'Ah was wid dem white chillum so much till Ah didn't know Ah wuzn't white till Ah was round six years old. Wouldn't have

found out then, but a man come long takin' pictures'"
(Hurston 8–9). Innocently, Janie asks: "Where is me? Ah don't
see me" (9). Such examples show that there are situations in
which the disenfranchised female is not cognizant of herself
and her enslaved state.

In the second stage, "Consciousness," the journey to female
awareness starts with the black female recognizing her status
and marginalization in white patriarchal society. Harriet Jacobs
learns of her slave status after her mother dies (6). It is only
when another asks the character Janie, "'Dat's you, Alphabet,
don't you know yo' ownself?'" that she realizes that she is black
(9). With this new knowledge of her forced marginality, Janie,
like Linda Brent, realizes that her "place" is the same as her
grandmother's: to serve and be exploited by others. This ele-
ment of difference begins for the female an interrogation of her
racial identity. In some situations, the process begins immediately when the black female realizes that her racial difference lies
in her assigned position, which is notably different from that of
her white counterpart. The "Consciousness" stage, as in slave
narratives, often begins at puberty and is much like the one
Harriet Jacobs experiences when realizing that she is unlike the
whites around her. The female in this case understands that
whites also view her as remarkably different from the privileged
white female. Though patriarchal European/European American
societies idealize the white female as the virtuous "true woman,"
the young black female, nonetheless, works to remain focused
on what is expected of her by the African American women in
her life and the black community in which she lives.

Because African Americans are derived from various backgrounds and experiences, the moment or point from which
one's identity is constructed or realized is much more compli-
cated than a monolithic determination of racial and gender
identity. It might be too naïve to ascertain that the forming of
one's identity can be constructed precisely, in a manner of
speaking, by some rigid formula. At best, this work points to
and analyzes the patterns or moments of identity formation I
find in black female slave narratives and in stories centered on
instances of female enslavement. However, it is no revelation
that blacks, in this case African American women, used their

oppressive conditions and their knowledge of what it means to be black and female as a measurement of their "being" in unsafe spaces. Collins explains, "For U.S. Black women, constructed knowledge of self emerges from the struggle to replace controlling images with self-defined knowledge deemed personally important, usually knowledge essential to Black women's survival" (100). It is this self-knowledge that fuels African American women's determination to create new identities and subsist even when others would prefer their annihilation.

In cases of enslaved women, this self-knowledge was key for enduring the common sexual exploitation they experienced. The young black female, during the "Consciousness" stage, is often moved from her familial surroundings and parents' protection. For young slave girls, sexual assault usually begins at this point. Jacobs as characterized as Linda Brent in her narrative explains that the fifteenth year is "a sad epoch in the life of a slave girl" (27). Linda is reminded by the master's "foul words" when the mistress is not around. A common practice in slavery was that the young female slave was "force[d] to sleep in the same bedroom of the master or mistress, a situation which provided a convenient setting for sexual assault" (hooks, *Ain't* 25). Under constant threat of rape, she knows she is without the same protection granted to white women. Thus, the young female slave learns early that survival means her submissiveness and silence. In *Incidents in the Life of a Slave Girl*, Jacobs describes her first encounter with Dr. Flint and his "obsessive desire to assert his power over her" by constantly threatening rape. Jacobs writes, "I was compelled to live under the same roof with him—where I saw a man forty years my senior daily violating the most sacred commandment of nature. He told me I was his property; that I must be subjected to his will in all things" (27). To survive the risk of being assaulted and sold, Jacobs remains silent even when her suspecting mistress pressures her to reveal Dr. Flint's misdeeds. In *Behind the Scenes,* Elizabeth Keckley echoes Brent's sentiments of the life of an adolescent slave girl. However, Keckley, unlike Brent in her telling, provides her audience neither her sexual history nor accounts of the sexual assaults she experienced as an enslaved female. Fair-looking Keckley explains, "For four years a white man...had base designs upon me. I do not care to dwell upon this subject, for it is fraught with pain" (38–39). Even in her Post-reconstruction slave narrative, Keckley understands the risk for her personal safety and status as a true woman in disclosing the details of her master's assault. Remarkably, these women used silence as a form of resistance, which is derived from their awareness of their positions as unprotected female slaves. It is essentially this slave/master relationship that initiates and develops their realities as black women.

The third stage of the Transient Woman's progression is "Rebelliousness." No longer content with complacency and being satisfied with social negation and marginality, the female acts against her oppression. In this phase, the female moves to the center of dominant discourse and actively engages in combat with her oppressor. Escaped Sojourner Truth talks back to her white owner when he tells her that she must return. Truth's "decisive answer was, 'No, I *won't* go back with you'" (*Narrative* 29). In Jacobs' case, she challenges Flint's sexual advances by asserting her own rebelling will and chooses her own sexual partner by taking a white male lover. Keckley describes in her slave narrative, *Thirty Years a Slave*, how she resists a sexual assault and flogging by the white Mr. Bingham: "No Mr. Bingham, I shall not take down my dress before you. Moreover, you shall not whip me unless you prove the stronger. Nobody has a right to whip me" (33). No longer willing to remain submissive, Keckley and Truth as Transient Women assert themselves through what Fulton describes as black feminist orality "in which one responds with independence, knowing, and force to an individual in authority" (13). It is the very nature of their unruliness and resistance that eventually allows them to move from their physical and psychological bondage as enslaved women.

Following acts of disobedience, the Transient Woman in the fourth stage, "Flight," asserts herself and moves away from the place of oppression and difference. In her rebellious act of breaking away from her oppressor, she claims her right to move freely toward a fuller understanding of herself while casting off the identity imposed on her in slavery. As she moves from the margin, the Transient Woman journeys temporarily to unbound locations or what Homi K. Bhabha describes as the "beyond" that, I suggest, allows time for fully understanding and reclaiming the female self. Jacobs' "intervening space 'beyond,'" is in her grandmother's attic crawl space (*Location* 7). For bondswoman Truth, "beyond" space is her departure to the woods for supplication prior to going on the speaking circuit for abolishing slavery. Former slave Keckley takes refuge in St. Louis trying to buy time and freedom before her move to Washington. In the process of their affirming or claiming their selfhood, these women, like the Transient Woman, create their own "fluid status" in opposition to the one for which they are assigned in patriarchal space (William Andrews 179).

For the Transient Woman, "Beyond,"[17] as I employ it, allows for women to heal from the physical and psychological oppressions of race and gender. The concept of "safe" space, in the fourth stage of Flight, is necessary for African American women to affirm themselves and heal from patriarchal wounds of oppression. Chancy iterates this point in *Searching for Safe Spaces* (1997), arguing that "Instead of continuing to feed the male models of misogyny and female subjugation, Black feminists...have within their power to construct safe spaces for the nurturance of women's lives, free of...the prejudices of racism and sexism" (124). Pointing to black feminists who have the resources to redirect African American women's efforts, Chancy understands that it takes the communal effort of black women to place their experiences at the center of any discourse.

Although the movement of the Transient Woman occurs within spaces where the female refuses to be subordinated, she does not, however, remain alone or indefinite in the realm of "Beyond." Black women do transition back into society to practice what they learned through black female consciousness. In safe space or women-centered location, black women assume a "womanist" perspective and are vigilant in not practicing separatism and/or possessing utopian views.[18] Self-definition and self-empowerment are exercised when women collectively express and practice their changed female consciousness within and at the center of dominant discourse. Lorde points out "For it is through the coming together of self-actualized individuals…that any real advances can be made" (46). Progress, then, according to Lorde, is one that is affirmed by women with like ideas for promoting black womanhood.

In the final phase in the Transient Woman's movement, Reentry or Materialization, the black female subject emerges from "beyond" or safe space to assert female agency and independence. The complete movement of the Transient Woman— Materialization or Reentry in the fifth phase—occurs when the female moves back to a world in which she can exert control and self-definition on her own terms. Specifically, self-definition "speaks to the power dynamics involved in rejecting externally, defined controlling images of Black womanhood" and to how African American women should act or perform (Collins 114). Such an example is when Sula in Toni Morrison's *Sula* returns to the Bottom after ten years and exercises her agency in being her own person. Rejecting the social notion of women having to marry, Sula responds cynically to her grandmother Eva Peace who asks, " 'When you gone to get married? You need to have some babies. It'll settle you' " (Morrison 92). Sula retorts, " 'I don't want to make somebody else. I want to make myself' " (92). After living independent of her grandmother and the black community that earlier judged her eccentricities, Sula learns that she must first know and define who she is before she can "make" another person. Similarly, Hurston's Janie returns to Eatonville, the town that had passed judgment on her as being "uppity" and orders the standards by which she will live as a changed woman. After spending time in a place where she developed into her own person, she comes back to exercise black femaleness after she had "been tuh de horizon and…now kin set…in [her] house and live by comparisons" (Hurston 182). Janie is not concerned with how others define and evaluate her against the ideal "good" or virtuous woman. By her own agency, she asserts her autonomy through her rejection of a socially acceptable image of womanhood and instead lives by her own standards learned in the "Beyond." The emergent stage, as portrayed in these examples, completes the Transient Woman whose experiences in the "Beyond" shows African American women in control of their lives.

The Transient Woman's movement back into society is not always successful. In some cases, after moving to a changed consciousness, the female subject does not make the complete circle in returning to "Beyond" or Third Space[19] for renewal and regeneration. After the black woman realizes the five stages toward new black female consciousness, she is required to return to the location where she first developed a changed view of her identity. The problems for her in society persist and recur even after she reasserts herself and fights back. To carry on in the struggles of racism and sexism, she must return periodically to safe space to reinforce what she has learned during her movement as Transient Woman. The real test of her change is whether she can survive in the same environments after having arrived at a new black female consciousness.

Identity and Self-Actualization

These stages, as conceptualized in the Transient Woman idea, correlate ideas of identity constructions and demonstrate how these formations of identity are an "important stage in liberation process" (hooks, *Yearning* 19). As mentioned, pinpointing the moment when one's identity is constructed can be difficult. However, slave narratives provide some notion as to how former slaves actualize their "being" through the act of "speaking" and "writing" the black self into existence. A majority of slave autobiographies, for example, commence with the narrator beginning with "I" or "I was born." The emphasis is deliberate in the action of the narrator in creating the "I" as a real person with personal history. In giving his version of his role as leader in the infamous 1831 slave revolt, Nat Turner begins his account by establishing his history as a man. He asserts, "I was thirty-one years of age the 2d of October last, and born the property of Benj. Turner, of this county" (Turner 44). Mary Prince in her narrative declares, "I was born at Brackish-Pond, in Bermuda, on a farm belonging to Mr. Charles Myners. My mother was a household slave; and my father, whose name was Prince, was a sawyer belonging to Mr. Trimmingham, a ship-builder at Crow-Lane" (Prince, *Six Women's Narratives* 1). Mattie Jackson establishes her history going further back in claiming herself as African. She writes, "My ancestors were transported from Africa to America at the time the slave trade flourished…My great grandfather was captured and brought from Africa. . . . My grandfather was born in the same state [New York]" (Jackson, *Six Women's Narratives* 5). What is important to note in these instances is the fact that blacks used orality and literacy to write and speak themselves into subjecthood and that the experiences are of a specific individual and not those of an object of possession.

For antebellum blacks, subjectivity is both a declarative act and a political act in the use of speaking and writing to declare themselves as men and women. Jacqueline Jones Royster makes clear the significance of blacks taking authority in advancing personhood. Royster writes, "What should be noted in particular is that, included in these actions, is the act of claiming thereby, with a sense of vision and agency, using literacy both well and with persuasive intent" (61). This is particularly significant as African Americans were cognizant that if there were possibilities for freedom and citizenship, social and political advancement had to begin with them first.

Using their experiences as slaves for knowledge, African Americans created what Jones describes as "a *working sense* of their environment and how to function within it" (59). Thus, blacks, in this case African American women, created their ideas of reality while at the same time understanding their places and making sense of the world they lived in. Recognizing her place as an enslaved woman, Harriet Jacobs in her narrative appeals to a white audience to understand the slave's afflictions, particularly the sexual assaults placed on the slave woman. She writes: "I have not written my experiences in order to attract attention to myself; on the contrary, it would have been more pleasant to me to have been silent about my own history" (1). Here, Jacobs, as writer, builds a case of herself as a decent person first, presenting an intelligent and well-meaning woman.

In creating an authentic self, slave narrators such as Jacobs testified to the truthfulness of their life stories while simultaneously declaring themselves as persons. Jacobs writes to her friend Amy Post: "I have My dear friend—Striven faithfully to give a true and just account of my own life in slavery. . . . I have placed myself before you to be judged as a *woman*" (my emphasis, *Incidents* xiii). Further, in the Preface of her autobiography, Jacobs asserts that her life story "is no fiction" and that it is "strictly true" (1). Frederick Douglass provides an example of his self-authorization and truthfulness in his reflection on a turning point of his life. Douglass avows, "I may be deemed superstitious and even egotistical, in regarding this event as a special interposition of divine Providence in my favor. But I should be false to the earliest sentiments of my soul, if I suppressed the opinion. I prefer to be true to myself, even at the hazard of incurring ridicule of others, rather than to be false, and incur my own abhorrence" (39). For Douglass, truth takes precedence over his audience's thoughts. Douglass's act in claiming "his allegiance to the self" is an "act of self-liberation" (103) in authorizing a claim to the self—an identity as man.

The enlistment of the self through rhetorical expressions of speaking and writing, as shown in slave narratives, is an example of a sociopolitical act of declaring the "self" into being. By insisting on a place for truth—authenticity of self—blacks constructed and actualized whole new "identities" outside the one that denied them subjectivity. Lorde makes clear the importance of exercising the whole self in view of hegemony's history of control. Regarding the importance of the whole self in the process of self-defining, Lorde writes,

> My fullest concentration of energy is available to me only when I integrate all the parts of who I am, openly, allowing power from particular sources of my living to flow back and forth freely though all my different selves, without the restrictions of externally imposed definition. (121)

Thus, the deed of declaring the whole self into being is a necessary act toward selfhood that resists invisibility and challenges all notions of objectification.

Gloria Anzaldua's New Mestiza Consciousness

The idea of the Transient Woman, in relation to female consciousness, complements Anzaldua's New Mestiza in *Borderlands La Frontera*.[20] In their effort to fight destruction of women's autonomy by social, economic, and political ideologies, both models support female development. Anzaldua's concept of the New Mestiza consciousness comes from what she sees as a problem as a result of the U.S.-Mexican war and the annexation of Texas—"a new U.S. minority: American citizens of Mexican descent" (Sonia Saldivar-Hull 2). Using this history and the rigid boundaries of race and gender, Anzaldua's celebration of the "mestiza consciousness" is closely linked with the Transient Woman's commitment to transformation and survival. As with black women, mestizas too must develop oppositional acts in the process of (re)creating and (re)defining a new mestiza's identity.

The split in living or having two cultures—Indian in Mexican culture and Mexican in white culture—presents problems for the mestiza.[21] As a consequence, in her dual existence, she holds two modes of living and thinking—as Indian and Mexican. The problem for her in existing in an oppositional culture, with two identities, is the issue W. E. B. DuBois identifies as double consciousness. In the case for African Americans, it is the internal conflict of living as black and American simultaneously and then the potential problem of conforming to an identity ordered by hegemony. The issue of double consciousness for blacks is the one that Anzaldua argues is a problem for the mestiza in her dual identity as Indian and Mexican in white patriarchal society. To heal the split, according to Anzaldua, the mestiza must move through four required stages for transformation that she outlines in *Borderlands*. Each phase is a process toward a New Mestiza consciousness that Anzaldua sees fundamental and necessary for the mestiza's survival.

The first begins in the rebellious phase called *Movimientos de rebeldiz y las culturas que tradicionan* ("Rebellious Movements and Traitorous Cultures"). Here, Anzaldua asserts, the mestiza confronts white and male dominance that restricts Chicano women. In the second stage, the *Coatlicue* State, the mestiza begins an understanding of the barriers that restrict her existence as a mestiza woman. The change in the mestiza's consciousness of moving away from any proscribed notion of female identity is actualized only when she faces her fears of her dual existence and then consciously makes the changes that will validate her identity as Mexican and Indian. This New Mestiza consciousness, Anzaldua asserts, comes from the mestiza's confronting and disrupting the "subject-object" duality of her old female existence in two cultures. Having experienced states of pain and distress, Anzaldua asserts the mestiza can no longer remain in her old state of being after coming into her new female knowledge. Anzaldua writes, "Knowledge makes me more aware, it makes me more conscious. 'Knowing' is painful because after 'it' happens I can't stay in the same place and be comfortable. I am no longer the same person I was before" (70). To create a new identity in the way she behaves and sees herself in the world, the old mestiza must question her old existence on the margin and radically establish a new way of feeling and knowing—the New Metiza consciousness (102).

Emerging from "a spiritual and political crossing" (7), the mestiza moves to the recovery phase, or what Anzaldua identifies as "The Mestiza Way." Here, the mestiza "take[s] inventory," which Anzaldua calls "put[ting] her history through a sieve" (104). The new and evolving mestiza takes time and examines closely those parts of herself that constitute "the baggage" from her ancestors. And then, as Anzaldua asserts, the mestiza consciously "takes on the struggle for social change" (7). Anzaldua writes,

> The step is a conscious rupture with all oppressive traditions of all cultures and religions...She reinterprets history...She strengthens her tolerance (an intolerance) for ambiguity. She is willing to share, to make herself vulnerable to foreign ways of seeing and thinking. She surrenders all notions of safety, of the familiar. Deconstruct, construct....She learns to transform the small "I" into the total Self. (105)

Anzaldua explains that in the process of looking at her history on the borders, the New Mestiza consequently recreates and reconstructs her identity in order to survive in the "borderlands." The New Mestiza is ever faithful in her task to "transform" and is prepared to tear down in order to build up a new way of thinking and believing outside the "small" self that would keep her on the margin.

In the final stage described as El Retorno, or the Return, "mestizas [are called] to action as they become [more] aware of multiple positionalities, contradictions, and ambiguities. The mestiza with her hard-earned consciousness cannot remain within the self" (Saldivar-Hull 12). As a consequence, activism is required on the mestiza's part. Because of her knowledge of past "borderland existence," the mestiza with her new mestiza consciousness is encouraged to fight against and resist living on the borders, again as the old mestiza.

Anzaldua's feminist approach to articulating a new consciousness for the mestiza is an appropriate paradigm for women of Mexican-Indian culture. Anzaldua reinscribes for Mexican-Indian women what is lost in colonization—her Mexican femaleness and mestiza identity. For Anzaldua, the answer to acculturation is "a massive uprooting of dualistic thinking in the individual and collective consciousness is the beginning of a long struggle" (102). No longer must mestizas struggle alone in saving their personal history as Mexican and Indian, instead they are joint in the task of saving their social and personal selves.

While the history and experiences of African American women are different from that of Mexican-Indian women, each group's effort toward a changed consciousness is characterized by oppositional acts to transcend margins and borders rooted in oppressive hegemony practices; Chicano women *migrate* from borders while African American women *move* from boundaries that oppress. The movement on the part of both groups includes separating from white social order to redefine their female identities in places that allow "articulating *different*."[22] Because of their differences, particularly in social and political experiences, each takes a dissimilar route and emerges at the center of dominant discourse while realizing like results.

Homi K. Bhabha's Third Space

In regard to space and identity, the ideas of postcolonial cultural theorist Homi K. Bhabha play a significant part in helping to define and analyze the site in which African American women in this study begin the process of self-definition. Self-definition for black women happens in the now—the present—beginning in the space of social or "cultural difference." Cultural difference, according to Bhabha, occurs when cultures understand that difference is articulated

> in relation to that otherness internal to their own symbol-forming activity which makes them decentered structures—through that displacement or liminality opens up the possibility of articulating different, even incommensurable cultural practices and priorities. ("Interview" 210–211).

A culture or group realizes its disparity when it juxtaposes itself with another group or culture and then opens up the possibility of articulating difference. The location in which cultural difference is best conveyed, according to Bhabha, is in the notion of Third Space.

For black women, Third Space offers possibilities for a place and time from which black women can define their own terms by which they desire to be viewed. Third Space, as conceptualized by Bhabha, is an intervening space in which "the overlap and displacement of domains of difference—that the intersubjective and collective experiences of *nationness*, community interest, or cultural value are negotiated" (*Location* 2). Conceptually, Third Space, in the example of two cultures, is the intersecting of cultural differences. Social or cultural difference, in this case, is represented by the simultaneous ideology of hegemony and the representation of the marginalized. The overlapping of the two in Third Space is created in the "emergence of the interstices" or in the intervening spaces. These intervening spaces, as a result, allow for the emergence of newness in the form of what has already been identified by Bhabha as "*nationness*, community interest, or cultural value." Third Space, according to Bhabha, is a place for intervention or renegotiation of differences.

As a locale for redefining and renegotiating, Third Space is an ideal site for reconstructing African American women's histories and identities. Conceptually, Third Space as an intervening space permits the creation of new identities. Bhabha explains,

> The move away from the singularities of "class" or "gender" as primary conceptual and organizational categories, has resulted in an awareness of the subject positions—of race, gender, generation, institutional location, geopolitical locale, sexual orientation—that inhabit any claim to identity in the modern world. What is theoretically innovative, and politically crucial, is the need to think beyond narratives of originary and initial subjectivities and to focus on those moments or processes that are produced in the articulation of cultural differences. These "in-between" spaces provide the terrain for elaborating strategies of selfhood—singular or communal—that initiate new signs of identity, and innovative sites of collaboration, and contestation, in the act of defining the idea of society itself. (*Location* 1–2)

These new "in-between" spaces provide a beginning for the marginalized to reclaim their past history and to form new identities. In this setting, African American women who are moving toward black female consciousness can start the process of redefining black womanhood. The new black woman, as the Transient Woman, does not forget her past because it is her history of devaluation that moves her to the "beyond" in the processes of forming new identities.

Third Space, as I am using it in this study, is the link to the "Beyond," or the new unexplored space where African American women realize black female consciousness. Essentially, Third Space is a liminal holding place and the connector before the passage to the "center." The best example of how this works is a model similar to Bhabha's explanation of Third Space as a link to understanding cultural differences. To show the "in-between moment" in his model, he uses African American artist Renee Green's work, which shows the "binary logic through which identities of difference are often constructed—Black/White, Self/Other," and male/female (Bhabha, *Location* 3). Bhabha uses Green's metaphor of a museum building, where her work is displayed, to show Third Space as a link to understanding cultural difference in the "in-between moment." Bhabha quotes Green who says,

> I used architecture literally as a reference, using the attic, the boiler room, and the stairwell to make associations between the certain binary divisions such as higher and lower and heaven and hell. The stairwell became a liminal space, a pathway between the upper and lower areas, each of which was annotated with plaques referring to blackness and whiteness. (Green 4)

The "stairwell," in this example, becomes significantly important because it is a link to reach other places within the large dominating space of the museum. As a connector to the lower or higher places, the "stairwell" provides the mechanism to change or move from one's position within the larger setting. Without the stairway, the chances of moving to other locations without incurring some disruption are increasingly remote. The other key point about chances of delay in trying to move out from one space to another is that there is the real possibility of never getting there. Precisely in Petry's *The Street* and Larsen's *Quicksand* and *Passing*, female characters that lose sight of the necessary "tools" to battle female oppression—female consciousness and female bonds—unfortunately come to calamitous ends. Literally speaking, being unequipped to move from one space to another, in this case recognizing oppressive practices, can be catastrophic and fateful. Bhabha, in connection with Green's stairwell notion, explains the formation of new identities and its usefulness stating that

> the stairwell as liminal space, in-between, the designations of identity, becomes the process of symbolic interaction, the connective tissue that constructs the difference between the upper and lower, black and white. The hither and thither of the stairwell, the temporal movement and passage that allows, prevents identities at either end of it from settling into primordial polarities. This interstitial passage between fixed identifications opens up the possibility of a cultural hybridity that entertains difference without an assumed or imposed hierarchy. (*Location* 4)

As a linkage to new selfhood, Third Space acts as a channel in giving rise to something new and different—a new area of self-representation. It is here in this productive locale of difference that otherness is resolved and recreated away from and outside a "universalist framework" (209).

Conceptually, Bhabha's idea of Third Space as an intervening location is effective in describing the process through which African American women must negotiate black female consciousness and subjectivity. However, in this study, the process of self-definition extends Bhabha's notion of Third Space or the "beyond" to another site to which African American women travel and shows that they are not and cannot be fixed in this intervening space as he uses it. Thus, liminality for them is a conscious state of perpetual movement crossing and moving boundaries that restrict autonomy. Third Space, in this study, is a transitory site—a spiritual place for transformation. Part of the difference is also how this study utilizes the word "beyond," which is different from Bhabha's use in his ideal of Third Space. For Bhabha, Third Space is the "in-between" and the "beyond." This study, however, uses Bhabha's definition of what it means to "dwell 'in the beyond' " to define black women's Third Space and black women's "Beyond."[23] Using it to describe the other location to which black women travel, this work shows it as a site in the continual process to black female consciousness and subjectivity. Black women's Third Space reveals the place—an unexplored terrain—African American women must travel to in order to become new subjects after they have moved from the space of difference or the boundaries of Other.

African American women's literature affirms black women's efforts to redefine black womanhood. Particularly, the works show the common theme of women locating women-centered places for articulating black women's existence and identities outside powers that distort African American women's realities. To change the controlled and distorted images of African American women and to realize black women's autonomy, a radical change must take place within black female psyches in response to white dominant ideology. In the case of black female subjectivity, the transformation comes out of a changed black female consciousness regarding how African American women see themselves. When African American women realize a new consciousness, black female autonomy and self-determination will emerge. As Lorde asserts, patriarchal oppression cannot be dismantled by using the master's tools that perpetuate white male domination. The change for black women in this situation is realized when African American women "dwell in the Beyond," or in black women's Third Space, and define the terms by which they are judged. Toward this effort, this study considers and conceptualizes[24] the geographical locations and psychological spaces in which African American women writers and women realize black female identity and autonomy.

3

Location, Female Autonomy, and Identity in Pauline Hopkins's *Contending Forces*

The appropriation and use of space are political acts.
—Pratibha Parma[1]

These "in-between" spaces provide the terrain for elaborating strategies of selfhood—singular or communal—that initiate new signs of identity, and innovative sites of collaboration, and contestation, in the act of defining the idea of society itself.
—Homi K. Bhabha[2]

Pratibha Parma claims that the appropriation and use of space are political acts. This chapter argues that Pauline Hopkins's novel *Contending Forces* (1900) makes an important contribution to black feminist practices by utilizing space as political and transient sites for African American women's transformation and autonomy. The importance of her contribution comes from her exploration of a crucial set of issues that band together around the question of black female identity and position. These include the relationship between black women's identity and their marginalization, the meaning of their marginalization from their positions in dominant society, and the relationship of their identity by the interconnection of race and gender.

Although some have viewed Hopkins's novel as promoting middle-class values, I argue that *Contending Forces* is more than African American women aspiring to act white and fit the idea of the True Woman. As the story surrounds Sappho and the places where she finds renewal and strength, *Contending Forces* supports Collins's idea of safe spaces as essential for black women's resistance (100–101). Collins describes these spaces as prime sites "in resisting objectification as the Other" (101). At best, African American women recognize that, to have any hope of resisting the hegemonic definition, black women must construct locations for black female autonomy independent of white dominant ideology. *Contending Forces* portrays black women's resistance and the connection between African American women and women-centered spaces for self-definition and renewal.

"Resistance, at root," as Thich Nhat Hahn has noted, "must mean more than resistance against war." He says,

> It is a resistance against all kinds of things that are like war....So perhaps, resistance means opposition to being invaded, occupied, assaulted and destroyed by the system. The purpose of resistance, here, is to seek the healing of yourself in order to be able to see clearly....I think that communities of resistance should be *places* where people can return to themselves more easily, where the conditions are such that they can heal themselves and recover their wholeness. (*emphasis added*) (qtd. in hooks, *Talking* 3)

For places where others can heal from continual social assault, Hopkins supplies sites for resistance and a changed female consciousness. The Smiths' house, Sappho's room, the Women's Sewing Circle, and the New Orleans convent are such places for resistance, which exemplify locations Sappho Clark uses to oppose hegemonic views of African American women. In fact, these sites become for Sappho what hooks identifies as "homeplace," a place or site where black women can resist the labels and views of the outside world (*Yearning* 42).

African American women's history reveals the extent to which black women have worked to establish a place of security and safety from white domination. Accounts of female slave narratives show the importance of establishing for female slaves a homeplace "in the midst of oppression and domination...[,] a site of resistance and liberation struggle" (*Yearning* 42). Following hours of toil in the domestic household or in the fields, black women returned to their cabins literally and figuratively to nurture themselves and their families and to be nurtured. They cared for their children, men, and one another in ways that lifted their spirits to resist and fight for freedom. In *Incidents in the Life of a Slave Girl* (1861), Jacobs relates her memory of her family "liv[ing] together in a comfortable home; and though [they] were all slaves, [Jacobs] was so fondly shielded that [she] never dreamed [she] was a piece of merchandise" (5). Jacobs's comment refers specifically to the safety in the homeplace of her grandmother. In her grandmother's home and away from the master's house, Jacobs is protected from the constant reminder of white domination and her position as slave.

Likewise, novelist Paule Marshall remembers the security and refuge she found in her mother's kitchen. Outside white stereotypes, Marshall's mother and aunts, in women-centered spaces, resisted the devaluation of black women by sharing in the female stories that comforted, fed, and nurtured their souls and spirits. In her novel *Brown Girl, Brownstones* (1959), Marshall uses the physical structure of the brownstones, not just as buildings, but as "homeplace" for a "means of survival and defense" ("Sculpture" 82). In her examination of Marshall's development of distinct women characters and their interconnection with culture and society, Christian describes the brownstones as "embodiments of the community's will to overcome all obstacles, [and to create] a protective barrier between it and the hostile world" ("Sculpture and Space" 82). This constant concern and need for African American women to find places to analyze themselves and the oppressive conditions in which they live are recurrent themes in black women writings, such as in Hopkins's turn of the century *Contending Forces*.

In Hopkins's first novel, *Contending Forces: A Romance Illustrative of Negro Life North and South* (1900), the concerns of black women finding new locations to redefine themselves as self-empowered subjects are embodied in the young Sappho Clark, a temporary boarder in the Smiths' house. Sappho intensely loves the new freedom found in the Northern life in Boston where the possibilities to advance and promote herself are beyond anything she imagined. She is looking for a new life—an independent existence and freedom from judgment.

Within the context of this newfound location, space and identity interconnect as Sappho tries to adjust in a setting to self-renew and to restore.

As a black feminist novel, *Contending Forces* shows the locations within female-centered spaces that allow resistance to sexism and racism. Black feminism as a womanist concept is about finding ways and places to escape, resist, and oppose dominant discourses and its practices of oppression and subjugation. In this narrative, locating places to resist dominant ideologies that see African American women as "Other" is critical for the novel's black female characters' own self-definition. The story, in this case, is not only about finding locations of recreating and redefining the black female, it is also about the progression toward black female self-definition and female autonomy in which Sappho is engaged.

The issue of self-definition has been central to African American women since their legal enslavement. Because black women were historically defined as licentious and oversexed, African American women have had to fight against the assault on black womanhood. As women in slavery, black women had no control over their bodies and were subjected to constant sexual assault by white men. In the rare case when a slave girl could fight off the advances of the slave master, she did so to protect her womanhood. While whites did not hold African American women to the standards of white womanhood, black women held themselves accountable to being virtuous and respectful. Harriet Jacobs, in writing her slave narrative, recounts the reaction of her grandmother when she discloses her pregnancy by her white lover, Mr. Sands. Feeling betrayed by Jacobs's decision to choose sexuality outside of marriage, the grandmother exclaims that she would rather see Jacobs dead than see her disgrace her black womanhood. Clearly, Jacobs's grandmother and other African Americans at the time held their own to the same standards of nineteenth-century womanhood.

The efforts of African American women in defining and examining black female self-definition are expressed as a prominent theme in early black women's autobiography and writing. For example, in recreating herself as a person and woman, former slave Isabella Van Wagenen renames herself Sojourner

Truth (Truth 68). The act of renaming is revolutionary as Truth reorders and reconstructs her own identity. Then in her famous speech at the Women's Rights Convention in Akron, Ohio, Truth publicly asserts and answers that like her white counterparts, she is a woman. Refusing to be defined by others and held up as "The Libyan Sibyl," Truth denies the abstract statue symbol created as a representation of her by William Wetmore Story and Harriet Beecher Stowe. In a similar manner, Francis E. W. Harper in her novel *Iola Leroy, Shadows Uplifted* (1892) recreates and transforms the tragic mulatto as portrayed in white fiction in the nineteenth century. Unlike the tragic female figure in sentimental fiction who succumbs to tragedy and dies, Harper's Iola Leroy defies the meaning of tragic mulatto and remains true to her black female identity and survives. Similarly, for Zora Neale Hurston, black women's self-definition is determined through her fictional characters Janie Crawford and Missie May. Writing in a discreet way to keep her female characters from being labeled licentious women, Hurston defends and celebrates black female sexuality in showing Janie and Missie May feeling comfortable with their sexual bodies.

To oppose the dominant ideology of black women, African American women must move toward black female self-definition in places where a community of resistance is possible. Female self-definition is the conscious will on the part of a woman to define herself by her own terms and not by others' values, beliefs, and expectations. When she does, she creates female autonomy by setting the conditions by which she lives and experiences life. No longer comfortable looking at herself through the eyes of others, a black woman purposely and defiantly constructs her own vision for self-knowledge and autonomy in sites with other women, countering negative images of black women. "Self is not defined as the increased autonomy gained by separating oneself from others," as Collins observes; "instead self is found in the context of family and community" (113). When linked by a common bond and agenda with women like them, the struggle for self-definition and autonomy provides for a deeper and more meaningful definition of black womanhood.

BLACK FEMALE DEVELOPMENT IN
CONTENDING FORCES

Hopkins's *Contending Forces* is an expansion of the theme of African American women moving toward self-definition within the context of place. That Hopkins is a political activist, as duCille asserts, "*Contending Forces* is an act of resistance and intervention" (36). The novel's preface makes clear her aim and insists that African Americans must find the means by which to define themselves. Hopkins writes, "We must ourselves develop the men and women who will faithfully portray the inmost thoughts and feelings of the Negro with all the fire and romance which lie dormant in our history" (36). "By no means is the novel a little romance" (duCille 36). Clearly, Hopkins is referring to the need of African Americans—in this instance, black women writers—to describe and render faithful pictures of a true black woman. Regardless of past critics' assessment of Hopkins's text, Hopkins's novel is at the center a discussion of female subjectivity and situates black women in sites and positions to author and interpret their own realities. Precisely, they become empowered subjects rejecting biased and negative contrasting past images of themselves.

A major part of the novel, featuring places of female resistance and development, is constructed in four locations: Ma Smith's Lodging-House, Sappho's room, the Sewing Circle, and the New Orleans convent. Placing black women in contained locations, Hopkins uses these sites to stage the role and effect of female-centered places, and the function of black women as a community among themselves. Hopkins begins her assessment of sites for black female realization in Ma Smith's Lodging-House. The site of the Smiths' house helps in the discussion of places of resistance because it is socially similar to the living arrangement in slave quarters and communities. Where those who lived under a common roof were often not related, the dwelling place served as "home" to the many displaced by slavery. By definition, these homeplaces were safe spaces; they were shared by those who were alike in race and social status. "Home" was safe because the inhabitants were free from the scrutiny of the dominant culture. Here, in shared space, blacks established community through like ideas for survival and endurance.

The Smiths' Lodging-House consists of the Smith family and several boarders who are "respectable though unlettered people"; Hopkins describes them as "possess[ing] kindly hearts and honesty of purpose in a greater degree than you find in a lodging-house" (102). They come from various backgrounds, but all carry the shared history of oppression. Having moved from places of suppression and fear, they come to the Smiths' house seeking new locations for freedom and independence. Mrs. Ophelia Davis and Mrs. Sarah Ann White, both born and raised in slavery, seek new beginnings with the hope of a laundry business partnership. Others include William Smith's companion (John Langley), an aspiring lawyer, a young student preacher from the "first square-back," two dressmakers from the "second-front and back," and the young and beautiful Sappho Clark from the "second floor front" (106, 107). While members of the Smiths' house come from different backgrounds and live in different locations of the house, by definition they are a family and a community. Ira Berlin, Steven Miller, and Leslie Rowland note that African Americans, since African slavery, have understood their society "in the idiom of kinship" and as extended kinship outside bloodlines because slavery had forced families to live apart (85). Thus, in the nineteenth century, kinship ideology and practices from slavery continued in African American communities.

For slaves and newly freed people, the construction or idea of a homeplace had political connotations. As observed by hooks, "homeplace was the one site where one could freely confront the issue of humanization, where one could resist" (hooks *Yearning* 42). At the end of the day, having worked outside the security of the Smiths' house, the dwellers come together and take communion in Mrs. Smiths' prepared foods. " 'Good things to eat,' " said Ma Smith, " 'make a man [and woman] respect him[or her]self and look up in the world. You can't feel that you are nobody all the time if once in a while you eat the same quality of food that a millionaire does' " (Hopkins 103). Mrs. Smith's task of giving food to her boarders is not just about providing a service; it is about the creation of a secure place where they can affirm their identities as true men and women and "by so doing heal many of the wounds inflicted by racist domination" (*Yearning* 42).

In writing about contained safe spaces for the inhabitants of the Smiths' house at the turn of the century, Hopkins recognizes blacks' need for a space of their own for restoring the black psyche. The psyche is a particular part of one's spirit or soul within the physical body, the inner part of the spirit that has power, as described by Lorde, "to give us the energy to pursue genuine change...rather than settling...in the same weary drama" created by the outer world of racism and sexism (59). Hopkins's character Mrs. Ophelia Davis, who moves north at the end of the Civil War, exclaims, " 'yas'm, I'm tired o' livin' in white folkses' kitchens' " (105). With her friend Mrs. Sarah White, Mrs. Davis realizes that possibilities for change will materialize with those in Mrs. Smith's house. Because of Mrs. Smith's character in the community and the people surrounding her, with Mrs. Smith's "known respectability...they could there come in contact with brighter intellects" (104). Living and coming in contact with successful black boarders, Mrs. Davis and her companion are likely to succeed as well in changing the conditions of their lives.

hooks recognizes the importance of spaces to restore that part of the psyche minimized and destroyed by the dominant ideology and culture. In her essay "Homeplace," she writes,

> Black women resisted by making homes where all black people could strive to be subjects, not objects, where [they] could be affirmed in [their] minds and hearts despite poverty, hardship, and deprivation, where [they] could restore to [themselves] the dignity denied [them] on the outside in the public world. (*Yearning* 42)

In the dominant world, Mrs. Ophelia Davis and Mrs. Sarah White might always be viewed as "cooks" and "servant gals." But in Mrs. Smith's Lodging-House, they can restore to their inner being that part removed by oppression. In Ma Smith's house, they are self-empowered subjects making their own way in a society that attempts to minimize their worth as black women. The will of Hopkins's female characters—their search for whole identity—comes from Hopkins's contention that "from the lowliest walks of life we cull the hope of a future life beyond the perplexing questions of [their] present existence" (86). Regardless of their current conditions as ex-slaves and black women, Hopkins asserts that there are possibilities for change and new identities.

As a place for self-healing from her secret past, Sappho finds refuge and retreat in the Smiths' house. Little is known about Sappho's past, but the depiction of Sappho as a Transient Woman who moves across spaces is evidenced in Sappho's explanation of the personal items she carries with her into her new setting. Dora is quite surprised and taken with Sappho's use of simple furnishings to refurbish the plain room and expresses her astonishment with the transformation. Sappho explains, " 'I always carry these things with me in my *travels*, and I find that I can make myself very comfortable in a short time with their help' " (*emphasis added*) (Hopkins 99). Hopkins reveals that Sappho often moves and travels from place to place and carries her "things" to make her transition easy. The "things" she carries on her "travels" are read as Sappho's figurative female tools used for adjusting to new situations and locations. Indeed, as black feminists argue, black women must be properly equipped to deal with the constant reminders of their prescribed place in the world. It is reasonable that Sappho would be prepared with the "psyche gear" necessary for the success of her adjustment into the society she plans for a new life and identity.

Creating new identities calls for an understanding of the daily and common challenges to black womanhood. Like any person migrating to unknown places, that person will learn and employ strategies for surviving in places and situations unknown. These survival tactics in relation to one's familiarity of place or locale express Anzaldua's mestiza dual consciousness, which suggests that Sappho is living in two realities—one black, one white. Anzaldua explains, "Not only [i]s the brain split into two functions but so [i]s reality. Thus people who inhabit both realities are forced to live in the interface between the two, forced to become adept at switching modes" (59). In each place, the person learns to switch courses and responds in accordance with the location in which he or she exists.

For Sappho, having moved to the North to escape her past identity as Mabelle Beaubean, forming a new self is critical. Sappho's skill at moving around and away from issues that open up questions about her former life is exemplified when Dora complements Sappho on her embroidery and asks Sappho to teach her the skill. Though Sappho is happy to oblige Dora by teaching her the craft, Dora nevertheless "notice[s] that she did not tell her where she had learned [it]" (Hopkins 99). Sappho believes that, for the time being, keeping her personal history in the past is best. Innocently, Dora asks more questions in trying to find out about her past and to form a relationship with Sappho and continues to inquire about her work. Having been isolated in her past life, Sappho understands Dora's intentions and opens up to Dora: "'Oh, I like the work very well...But generally speaking, I prefer it to most anything that I know of. Do sit down'" (99). Because of her past, Sappho had preferred her work over cultivating meaningful relationships. Interestingly, Hopkins revises the nineteenth-century heroine who generally succumbs to the circumstance of a fallen woman and demonstrates that Sappho is "a virtuous person through the strength of her character" as an earnest and independent woman (Tate 161).

As a strategy to overcome her tainted history, Sappho projects herself as a self-reliant woman and revises the fate of a sexually violated woman. Black feminist thinker Maria Stewart, in her 1831 essay, encourages black women's self-definition as key to black women's survival in any situation:

> We have never had an opportunity of displaying our talents; therefore the world thinks we know nothing....Possess the spirit of independence. The Americans do, and why should not you? Possess the spirit of men, bold and enterprising, fearless and undaunted. Sue for your rights and privileges. Know the reason that you cannot attain them. Weary them with your importunities. You can but die if you make the attempt; and we shall certainly die if we do not. (38)

For Stewart, survival is directly related to black women "possess[ing] the spirit of independence" and being self-reliant. Clearly, African American women must learn to rely on their inner spirits and powers at the same time they encourage other black women to value self-determination. In this sense, domestic Dora is fascinated with Sappho's independence, courage, and career in a life away from family or other support. In Sappho, Dora "discover[s] a character of sterling worth—bold, strong, and ennobling" (Hopkins 114). Possessing characteristics usually exhibited in a nineteenth-century male, Sappho is unlike any other woman Dora has known.

Such an independent lifestyle for a woman was uncommon and not encouraged in the nineteenth century. A proper or True Woman remained within the boundaries of home that usually provided male protection. As "true women," females at the turn of the twentieth century were nevertheless expected to be pure, pious, submissive, and domestic. Subjected to the boundaries of domestic space, African American women, like their white counterparts, were bounded by parameters that allowed little if any female self-development. Early Black feminist Anna Julia Cooper advances her reaction to this condition: "Let our girls feel that we expect something more of them than that they merely look pretty and appear well in society" (Cooper 78). Seeing Sappho as a self-sufficient woman, Dora has "a great fascination…about the quiet, self-possessed woman" (97) and recognizes that a relationship with Sappho will "fill a long-felt want in her life" and for the first time she trusts her feminine intuition (Hopkins 98). This scene allows the novel to draw on what Lorde suggests is the need between women to nurture each other and it is there that their "real power is rediscovered." Lorde asserts, "Interdependency between women is the way to a freedom which allows the *I* to *be*, not in order to be used, but in order to be creative" (111). Undoubtedly, a relationship between Sappho and Dora will not only allow for self-renewal and development but also provide for "deeper, more meaningful self-definitions" (Collins 113).

Locations and Sites for
Female Transformation

The precise relationship between locations for black female development and female subjectivity is evident in Sappho's physical room. Sappho's room figuratively becomes a place for self-change and the recovery of a black female psyche. Lorde articulates that black women must change the conditions of their lives in order to be free and to be creative (111). She writes, "The master's tools will never dismantle the master's house. They may allow us temporarily to beat him at his own game, but they will never enable us to bring about genuine change" (Lorde 112). In this assertion, Lorde explores how independence and self-definition encourage black women to bring about social and personal change. Change will not materialize by resorting to the principles used by hegemonic power. On the contrary, change becomes possible when black women take control of their lives and set the conditions by which they will live while moving away from judgments of the hegemony. Thus, in the process of transforming the negative beliefs and perspectives about themselves, African American women can move beyond the parameters of white patriarchal ideology of black womanhood.

Significantly, Hopkins's use of separate space or location to connect with the female psyche reflects the same theme of defining the black female self that appears in Larsen's *Quicksand* (1928) and Hurston's *Their Eyes Were Watching God* (1933). By moving their heroines outside places that render them powerless, Larsen and Hurston show black female self-definition and female wholeness. As Transient Women, Helga Crane in *Quicksand* and Janie Crawford in *Their Eyes Were Watching God* demonstrate the importance of moving into both the psychological and the physical spaces for female consciousness and renewal. Each character accesses power for control of her destiny in the choices she makes once she recognizes the oppressive forces that disregard her existence. However, the prominent difference between the heroines of these texts is captured when each moves back to her former location after a temporary break or retreat from hegemonic space. Returning from a place of renewed consciousness, Janie, unlike Helga, rejects material possessions and social status and attains unquestionable autonomy. Likewise, Hopkins's novel traces the use of location for female autonomy and a changed female consciousness through her character Sappho Clark.

Using Sappho's room in the Smiths' house, Hopkins provides the space for connecting with the female psyche and for female bonding. In the beginning, Dora is not one who desires or seeks female friendship. "As a rule," she abstains from "girl friendships, holding that a close intimacy between two of the same sex was more than likely to end disastrously" (Hopkins 97–98). Learning from experience, Dora has distrusted relationships with women. To become a whole subject—that is, to encompass freewill in thought and movement toward black female consciousness—Dora's selfhood requires beginning a girlfriendship with Sappho. Feeling a stirring in her inner self, Dora recognizes that "she ha[d] from the first a perfect trust in the beautiful girl" (98). Perhaps, in other open locations of the Smiths' house, this awareness may not have been realized by Dora. But in Sappho's room, a woman-centered location, Dora changes her perspective about female relationships.

Dora and Sappho find in each other a yearning, or a missing part of themselves, while centering themselves in a location that allows female bonding. In Sappho's room or space, Dora finds in Sappho characteristics that she desires for herself; looking beyond Sappho's inner and outer beauty, Dora finds resilience and strength in female character. At the same time, "lonely self-suppressed" Sappho discovers in Dora the unrestrained spirit she lacks. Sappho observes in Dora an "energetic little Yankee girl swept like a healthful, strengthening breeze" (114). In anticipation of Dora's friendship, Sappho fleetingly forgets her past as she sees now a "new joy in living" (114).

Hopkins's chapter "Friendships" foregrounds the issues of girlfriendship, self, and location that become an important part of an understanding of Sappho's and Dora's move to black female subjectivity. Much of the action exerted by the two female characters in this chapter centers on their interactions with each other. Until Dora and Sappho bond, each appears content, but it is not until they become "girlfriends"[3] that each acquires something from the other that was missing in her life. With Dora, Sappho experiences perhaps for the first time a girlfriendship. Having been secluded from others, Sappho finds that the female connection with Dora is inviting, clear, and meaningful. When Sappho first moves to the Smiths' house, she fills her time exerting herself as she "generally carried her work home in the morning, [and] ten o'clock would find her seated at her desk and ready to begin her task anew" (115). But with Dora as her friend, Sappho "learn[ed] from observation the great plan of life as practiced in an intelligent, liberty-loving community" (115). Dora is Sappho's link to a refreshed self and a new identity. Each provides the other what the other is missing.

While constructing a bond with a like model of herself, Dora begins to engage black female subjectivity with her "female other" and self. Dora's life had focused on the familial, and so she had had few intimate female friends. Now she takes satisfaction in "watching the changes on the mirror-like face of her friend," Sappho (115). This mirrored image reveals that Dora is arriving at her own subjectivity by gazing at her likeness in Sappho. Dora and Sappho are the same, yet separate. From their separateness, each holds to her own uniqueness as woman that allows for her "selfness" to generate or remake herself. In their sameness, they share the same history as black women in locating their identities post-Reconstruction. Dora observes or recognizes her own self through Sappho. Kevin Everod Quashie understands the "solidarity of girlfriend subjectivity" as a process and is totally committed to focusing on the lives and experiences of black women (16); in "The Other Dancer as Self," he claims,

> [A] subject's desire and impulse toward an/other is political, aware of but not overdetermined by the legacies of race, gender, and class; it is sisterhood as "political solidarity between women." This solidarity is not a state of achievement but, rather, a process, and it extends beyond its own specificity such that the power of negotiating otherness between two Black women is both a model and conduit for a Black female subject's (un)becoming in relation to others who are not, in name, Black women but with whom she shares an ethical and political affinity. (16)

In the stages of actualizing selfhood, Dora as a black female connects *with* and becomes the same *as* her friend Sappho.[4] What is significant in this relationship is that achieving or materializing subjectivity is not only about an awareness of self in relationship to others in power but also about centering on female community as an important link in the process to selfhood. It is evident, as Quashie asserts, "that community is a particular location of power and self-identity for Black women" (16).

The description Hopkins offers of Sappho's and Dora's relationship as girlfriends is described by Quashie as "that of woman-centered engagement" (18) and advances the idea of women finding female identity and support in separate spaces: "On stormy days the two girls would sit before the fire in Sappho's room and talk of the many things dear to women, while they embroidered and stitched" (Hopkins 116). These times were special for connecting, relating, and bonding. They were essential for black women to sustain themselves against oppressive forces. As a professional stenographer, Sappho is not allowed to work in white public places; therefore, she brings her work home. However, even though, she must work at home, Sappho's and Dora's times together in support of the female other provide security from racism and sexism outside their existence. Hopkins writes, "By eleven o'clock they had locked the door of Sappho's room to keep out all intruders" (117). The women understand the forces that oppress, dominate, and negate women of color. In the act of "lock[ing] the door," Sappho and Dora, within a female-centered location, construct a safe space for nurturing black female consciousness and subjectivity by obliterating the forces that attempt to suppress them.

Politically, this description of black female subjectivity is conversant with Toni Morrison's *Sula* (1982), in which Nel and Sula locate literal and figurative spaces to actualize their oneness and yet realize their own "selfness" in bracing themselves against the world:

> So when they met…they felt the ease and comfort of old friends. Because each had discovered years before that they were neither white nor male, and that all freedom and triumph was forbidden to them, they had set about creating something else to be. Their meeting was fortunate, for it let them use each other to grow on. (56)

The idea of the young females experiencing and renewing the contentment of "old friends" suggests that they are reaching back and pulling forth the familiarity of "self"—the black female self. Uniquely, their identities as black and female allow each to sustain and develop from what each brings to the relationship.

Alice Walker's *The Color Purple* provides another example of how freedom of self and interactions in a women-centered place of confident women become one woman's freedom from suppressed female sexuality and identity. In female-contained spaces, Celie discovers her sexuality as Shug encourages her "to take a mirror and go look at [her]self" (77). Surprisingly, Shug is the one who helps Celie shed her insecurities about her female body. Christian reveals that "the love/sex relationship between Celie and Shug is...presented as a natural, strengthening process through which both women, as well as the people around them, grow" ("Trajectories" 246). In *The Color Purple*, Walker exposes the naturalness of female intimacy, as does Hurston with Janie and Phoeby in *Their Eyes* and Hopkins with Sappho and Dora.

The assumption of "safe spaces" as locations for female development opens for inquiries. Why separate spaces? What, if any, are its limitations for female progress? Do boundaries restrict selfhood? How do female spaces or "communities" produce change in the female self? Do boundaries or separate locations make a significant difference in developing or constructing black female autonomy? In raising these questions, I bring attention to how African American women have resisted and created new locations for defining themselves outside the measuring and monitoring by others. Despite the constraints of race, sex, and class, African American women "have not been thoroughly neutralized or contained" (Royster 4). From black women's autobiography and literary works, the reality we come to know is that black women have found ways in new locations "to break out from...containments [that] would seek to enclose them" (4). Thus, my endeavor here is to explore and investigate how African American women have traversed unfriendly landscapes in which they have, through community deliberateness, attained and manifested black female selfhood.

Understanding the dissimilarities between spaces imposed by one's own self and boundaried spaces enforced by others is to see the value and function of these politicized sites. The major difference linking the two is the matter of choice. To construct consciously places or boundaries away from others is a radical act or move. To do so is to recognize differences of race, gender, and class and the constraints placed on the female psyche by the hegemony. The move to less-inhibited spaces is an essential one, particularly for African American women. Black women, Lorde asserts, "have been taught either to ignore [their] differences . . . than [recognize them] as forces for change" (112). She explains,

> Those of us who stand outside the circle of this society's definition of acceptable women; those of us who have been forged in the crucibles of difference—those of us who are poor, who are lesbians, who are Black, who are older—know that *survival is not an academic skill*. It is learning how to stand alone, unpopular and sometimes reviled, and how to make common cause with those others identified as outside the structures in order to define and seek a world in which we can all flourish. It is learning how to take our differences and make them strengths. *For the master's tools will never dismantle the master's house.* (Lorde 112)

Instead of cowering and accepting the perspectives of others in the devaluation of black female identity, African American women have choices, in different sites and locations, to make change. Within the safety of female community, they are free to deny male models of power and to empower themselves by constructing their own female identities. Hopkins's treatment of places—particularly the use of Sappho's room, the Women's Sewing Circle, and the convent in the South—indicates that women have places of their own for female self-realization. As sites for reacting to white patriarchal views, these locations facilitate the development of black female identity.

Intervening Sites for Female Consciousness

The Women's Sewing Circle serves as a transitory site where Sappho and Dora develop black female consciousness in their move to female subjectivity. The women gathered in the back parlor of Ma Smith's house, ready to "perform any service which might be required of them" (Hopkins 143). Besides "putting garments together," the women meet to help their "race to help itself, along the lines of brotherly interest" (142). Even after a day of tireless working and caring for others, the women find time for female nurturance among themselves. In this space, Hopkins uses Ma Smith's back parlor for the women to discuss the subject of the "place which the virtuous woman occupies in upbuilding a race" (148), a space to define the true meaning of a virtuous black woman. Mrs. Willis, the leader of the women's group, begins the discussion of the significance of the black woman in the African American struggle by claiming black women's responsibility in changing the views of black women themselves:

> "I am particularly anxious that you should think upon this matter seriously, because of its intrinsic value to all of us as race women. I am not less anxious because you represent the coming factors of our race. Shortly, you must fill the positions now occupied by your mothers, and it will rest with you and your children to refute the charges brought against us as to our moral responsibility, and the low moral standard maintained by us in comparison with other races." (148)

Mrs. Willis urges black women to change their opinions about themselves. Even as she resolves that the future of the race lies with Sappho and the other young women, Mrs. Willis challenges them to disprove the stereotype of promiscuous black women that they have been falsely judged to be.

The value of women-centered space is prominent for the young orphaned Sappho's character building and for black women uplift. Having a space for building black female strength and identity is clear when Sappho, a victim of rape, asks Mrs. Willis for her opinion on black female moral responsibility. She asks: " 'Do you think, then, that Negro women will be held responsible for all the lack of virtue that is being laid to their charge today? I mean do you think God will hold us responsible for the *illegitimacy* with which our race has been obliged, as it were, to flood the world?' " (149 emphasis in original). In the security of female space, Sappho uses this opportunity to ask questions she would not be free to raise in a more public and so less protected environment. Such questions by Sappho are the same ones raised by Hopkins and other African American women in the nineteenth century. Hopkins's political intent to argue against the notion of black women as sexual temptresses is revealed in the novel's preface: "I am not actuated by a desire for notoriety or for profit, but to do all that I can . . . to raise the stigma of degradation from my race" (13). In utilizing the novelistic form, Hopkins can bring to light the unwarranted claims on black women's sexual history. "But through religious rhetoric and a claim of essential purity" (McCullough 105), the character Mrs. Willis releases black women from blame: "I believe that we shall not be responsible for wrongs which we have *unconsciously* committed, or which we have committed under *compulsion*. We are virtuous or non-virtuous only when we have a *choice* under temptation" (149). Hopkins, through Mrs. Willis, defends black womanhood and expresses African American women's innocence in a wrong for which they are not responsible.

Without the Sewing Circle's location and Mrs. Willis, it is unlikely that Sappho would have consulted a male clergy in the matter of exempting a victimized black woman from the blame of rape. Though Mrs. Willis concludes that women are not to blame for their rape, the community temple's Rev. John Thomas views the birth of mulattos from rape differently. School teacher Anna Stevens, a member of the group, remembering bitterly Rev. Thomas's opinion of the mulatto "race," comments,

> "I shall never forget my feelings . . . at certain remarks made by the Rev. John Thomas at one of his noonday lectures in the Temple. . . . He touched upon the Negro, and with impressive gesture and lowered voice thanked God that the mulatto race was dying out, because it was a mongrel mixture which combined the worst elements of two races. Lo, the poor mulatto! despised by the blacks of his own race, scorned by the whites! Let him go out and hang himself." (Hopkins 150)

The beliefs of Rev. Thomas represent the irony of African American women assuming any male/societal forgiveness for the act of rape. In the case of Anna Stevens, Rev. Thomas's views relay the general public's suspicion that it is the fault of the black woman for the "mongrel mixture" of the black and white races.

Contrasting Rev. Thomas's views, Mrs. Willis asks Anna if she thinks "the black race . . . has developed into a race of mulattoes?" (151). Mrs. Willis points out that "it is an incontrovertible truth that there is no such thing as an unmixed black on the American continent" (151). Her wisdom is more prominent when she tells the women that their lives will be "beautified and [the] race raised in the civilization" when they "*grow away from* all the[se] prejudices" in Boston [*emphasis added*] (Hopkins 152). Mrs. Willis brings up the history of the black race's success in renewing themselves after Reconstruction and states that the "thirty-five years of liberty have made [them] a new people" outside the dominant society that had viewed them as "inferior" (153).

Taking up Kate McCullough's point regarding Mrs. Willis's use of religious rhetoric in her discourse on black women, I assert that Mrs. Willis serves as a black female Moses. Hopkins positions Mrs. Willis as the black female spokesperson for African American women of the period. A widow left without money to support herself, Mrs. Willis is

> forced to begin a weary pilgrimage—a hunt for the means to help her breast the social tide. The best opening, she decided . . . was the great cause of the evolution of true womanhood in the work of the "Woman Question" as embodied in marriage and suffrage. She could talk dashingly on many themes. . . . The advancement of the colored woman should be the new problem in the woman question that should float her upon its tide into the prosperity she desired. And she succeeded well in her plans: conceived in selfishness, they yet bore glorious fruit in the formation of clubs of colored women banded together for charity, for study, for every reason under God's glorious heavens that can better the conditions of mankind. (Hopkins 146–147)

By working on the "Woman Question," Mrs. Willis serves both women and the African American race in racial uplift.

Mrs. Willis, like the biblical Moses, understands also the inherited power of her people in moving "away from" the prejudices of their time. While the "exodus" is not a physical one, Hopkins, through Mrs. Willis, shows that African Americans must undergo a psychological "exodus" to change their inner views and expectations of themselves. What is required, according to Hopkins, is a spiritual cleansing of the inner psyche, which is realized outside "a higher race" (153).

More than a place to discuss political and social views, the Women's Sewing Circle also provides the occasion for female bonding. In this arrangement, the Sewing Circle represents what McCullough calls "a united community of women" that signifies friendship and love. Embodiments of genuine care and sisterly love are exemplified by Mrs. Willis when she observes Sappho's anxious nature and tries to be encouraging: " 'If I can comfort or strengthen, it is all I ask' " (155). Mrs. Willis extends the definition of friendship and acts as counsel and mother to Sappho. When allowance for nurturing and community building exist, women from the margins are enabled to make what others see as difference their female strength.

In a place of female friendship, Sappho feels secure to ask questions related to her female sexuality and feelings of affection. While reflecting on the issue of moral responsibility and rape, Sappho is confused about female sexuality and passion and questions how the two can coexist for a virtuous woman. Sappho asks Mrs. Willis,

> How are we to overcome the nature which is given us? I mean how can we eliminate passion from our lives, and emerge into the purity which marked the life of Christ? So many of us desire purity and think to have found it, but in a moment of passion, or under the pressure of circumstances which we cannot control, we commit some horrid sin, and the taint of it sticks and will not leave us, and we grow to loathe ourselves. (154)

Understandably, carrying the woman's stigma of temptress, "Sappho reads passion as lust" (McCullough 105). Sappho's fear of her female sexuality and sexual feelings comes back and reflects an anxiety that comes out of the stereotype of the lascivious black female created by the dominant culture, a stereotype that provided an excuse for white male rape. If African American women showed signs of sexual feelings and desire, then they, according to white dominant order, were in some way responsible for their own rape. Surrounded by women who share like concerns about female sexuality in terms of expression, Hopkins's Sappho, in a female sphere, is free to examine and discuss black female sexuality without white and male criticism.

These female-made boundaries do not limit or restrain Sappho's and Dora's movement toward black female subjectivity within their black and female communities. As a counterargument to Tate's view that Hopkins "restricted Sappho's voice to private space, preventing her penetration into the public sphere of influence" (161), I argue that private space, in fact, strengthens and opens Sappho to assert herself politically and publicly in the black Boston community. Having discovered and discussed the constraints of race and gender in the Sewing Circle, Sappho and Dora understand what it means to give and reach out to others:

> They visited the home for aged women on M—Street, and read and sang to the occupants. They visited St. Monica's Hospital, and carried clothes, flowers, and a little money saved from the cost of contemplated Easter finery. They scattered brightness along with charitable acts wherever a case of want was brought to their attention. (Hopkins 129)

In their acts to help and work with others, Sappho and Dora help themselves in moving from the boundaries of domesticity. In the nineteenth century, as male-dominant forces hold women to limited domestic spaces, the act of crossing boundaries into social spaces is a radical act in constructing subjectivity. No longer restricted to the spaces that keep women subjected to men, women see and understand how social relations work, which makes a difference in how they react to those who attempt to suppress them in their act of autonomy.

Dora and Sappho move outside female-centered spaces to gain autonomy, taking up work that centers them in social relations outside family and within female circles. Dora takes a salaried position as organist for a black church. Sappho, on the other hand, provides service as a professional stenographer. Though Sappho's work is done in a domestic sphere, she nevertheless exemplifies autonomy as she "secretly supports dependents and is capable of arranging her own affairs…[, including] taking a long train journey alone" (McCullough 33). In both situations, Sappho and Dora move outside prescribed female work and sites and step into spaces that allow them interaction outside or at the center of social relations. Performing work outside the "home" space, Sappho and Dora indicate that they are actors with or in the center of social/power relations. Doreen Massey makes the argument:

> One of the most evident aspects of this joint control of spatiality and identity has been in the West related to the culturally specific distinction between public and private. The attempt to confine women to the domestic sphere was both a specifically spatial control and through that a social control on identity. Again "A woman's place?" illustrates this theme, by pointing to the specific (though not unique) importance of the *spatial separation* of home and workplace in generating dismay in certain quarters at women becoming "economically active." (179)

The matter of women moving outside the domestic sphere and taking a place in the center of society appears in other females' actions in the novel as well. Anna Smith, a member of the Sewing Circle, is a school teacher. Mrs. Ophelia Davis and her friend Sarah Ann, former slaves, are proprietors of "The First-class New Orleans Laundry" (106). In Ma Smith's boarding-house live two dressmakers who provide services to Boston women (107). Likewise, Hopkins, a professional woman, worked outside the home as a stenographer and as an editor of *Colored American Magazine,* a major African American journal. As editor, Hopkins was at the center of discussions surrounding race and politics, thus influencing the minds in black communities. Hopkins, in her novel, delineates new roles for women, underscoring that women are not naturally linked to the borders of home or domestic space.

Male Constraints on Female Development

Hopkins's *Contending Forces* reveals other restrictions on the black female psyche that hinders self-determination. Entrenched with deceit and sexual cruelty, John Langley's character makes it possible for Hopkins to comment on the importance of female knowledge or developed consciousness. Hopkins shows Sappho's naiveté when Langley tries to force her into a sexual liaison through a sexual proposition to keep her past a secret. Encouraging Sappho to believe that she has nothing to fear from him in revealing her secret past, Langley gives the impression that he is honorable in his intentions when he expresses to Sappho: "There are men in the world who would not forsake you, and who would always befriend you. *Give up Will, and trust yourself to me*...I can and will do well by you. Your story need never be known" (Hopkins 319). By such an assertion Langley, McCullough claims, "rehearse[s] a white dominant order's narrative of the fallen woman" (107) in her duty to make amends for her social and sexual past. Langley's reasoning also follows from slavery ideology in its view of African American women; Sappho is property to be bought and owned by men. With her secret revealed and Langley's threats, Sappho's whole being responds to her possible fate: "Nervous spasms shook [Sappho's] frame as she mentally measured the abyss of social ostracism and disgrace which confronted her" (320). Explicit here are the "contending forces" of a sexual scandal and racial attitude that could potentially destroy Sappho. For women in the nineteenth century, male dominance held the power of determining and naming women's state of being or condition in society.

In recognizing the power of men, John Langley understands how easily a woman can be pushed from her place in society by attempting to hold Sappho hostage to her past history. In Langley's misuse of power, Sappho is made a victim of race, gender, and class. As Sappho tries to regain her self from what was developing in her female psyche to survive, Sappho misappropriates her female knowledge in anger and thoughts of revenge:

> Sappho had suffered much in meekness, but now dumb rage awoke her passions. For a time the spirit of revenge held full sway in the outraged heart. Revenge was all she craved; she shivered at the dark thoughts which came to her. "Revenge" ... revenge

upon her reducer and upon the man who had dashed the cup of happiness from her lips and most wantonly insulted her in her weakness. (341–342)

While these heated emotions could lead to temporary reprisal for Sappho, Hopkins invites revision; Sappho relinquishes and transforms her anger into action to bring about a change to her condition in a temporary retreat to a southern convent. According to Lorde's use of anger, "anger expressed and translated into action…is a liberating and strengthening act of clarification, for it is in the painful process of this translation that we identify…who are our genuine enemies" (127). In Sappho's example, the use of anger allows her removal to another space to regroup and to aid her later in dealing with male confrontations about her past.

Although Sappho is a potentially tragic woman, Hopkins changes the fate of the naive Sappho and prevents her fall from nineteenth-century "True Womanhood." Twice in the story Hopkins alters Sappho's destiny by her movement away from situations and spaces that threaten her inner being. Unlike Grace Montfort, in the opening of the novel, who chooses death—in "the waters of Pamlico Sound" (71)—over living with the disgrace of rape, Hopkins's Sappho does not choose death. Instead, Hopkins allows Sappho to find other options for changing her past shame and subjective experience in white male culture.

Locating Female Sites for Resistance

As an act of resistance, Sappho shifts from the center of male social interaction in Boston to a safe space that allows for female renewal and transformation. In transplanting Sappho to this new space, Hopkins is not making Sappho new in terms of female purity but instead is removing Sappho from a corrupt male space set apart by financial and sexual greed. The other part in understanding the significance of separation from patriarchy is the necessity for Sappho and African American women of the time to be in touch with the "erotic" for female self-preservation.

A New Orleans convent, as a place of retreat from her past that has been tainted by rape, becomes for Sappho a transitory site for renewal. The sites discussed before are in the context of women-centered spaces for self-knowledge. Such places are critical, first, to understand the female self and, second, to be conscious of the problems of race and gender that impel African American women back to female-centered spaces for renewal. However, in times of distress, the female, or the Transient Woman, moves into intervening sites for regeneration.

Twice in the novel, Hopkins uses the convent as a site of intervention. This space is described by Bhabha as that which demands an understanding of the past and the present and how both become "part of the necessity…of living" (*Location* 7). The first time Sappho retreats there is after she is raped by her white uncle. Sappho takes refuge at the "colored convent at New Orleans, and…there in the care of the sisters.…*she die[d] when her child was born*" (261). It is with that metaphorical passing or death of Mabelle Beaubean that she takes a new life and form in the figurative birth of Sappho Clark. When she exits from this bound space of the convent, Sappho returns to the community, taking a new identity that allows her to be identified as a respected and independent woman.

The second occasion the convent provides sanctuary for Sappho is after she is exposed by Langley as the raped Mabelle Beaubean. Hopkins shows Sappho's assurance in the safety of the convent in the narrator's certainty: "So once again Sappho found a *refuge* in the convent in her time of dire necessity" (348 emphasis added). At the time of revision to become anew, Sappho uses the comfort and security of the convent. She thinks, " 'A long spell of low fever ensued, but to Sappho in her weakness the rest and comfort that came to her harassed mind was like sun and shade in a grassy glade of perfect peace' " (349). Like the mestiza who goes "down into" the *mictlan,* where she "connects with conscious energy" (71) in removing the residue of the past, Sappho, the Transient Woman, crosses over into Third Space, the convent, to replenish her female "erotic" to later emerge as a renewed subject. Hopkins shows that healing the female psyche in women-centered sites is continuous and that the Transient Woman continually seeks refuge when the female psyche needs replenishment.

As temporary protection, the New Orleans convent, an intervening site, allows her a space separated from male-dominated society to understand and reclaim her self. What is also significant in this location for renewal is that hints of materiality, propelled by excessive greed, are removed from the space in which transformation is actualized. Here, Sappho finds peace and tranquility in a space that allows for replenishment. The narrator describes Sappho's room at the convent as a place outside a system that defines anything good in terms of material value:

> A small, bare room…at the end of a long corridor.…[, t]he light from the soft Southern moon…making the room like the cloisters of heavenly mansions. To that quiet haven of rest the turmoil and bustle of life did not reach. There the dying, the sick, the convalescent lay undisturbed by the hurrying march of humanity. (350–351)

The imagery reveals a room absent and "bare" of an all-powerful patriarchy. The room at the convent provides healing for the "sick" and "dying" Sappho and releases her from the excessive and impossible demands of the True Woman as conceptualized by dominant power.

Because of her status as an African American "woman" and "object," Sappho finds in the realm of the convent, as female-centered space, a safe haven from male dominance and intrusion. This feeling of marginalization is demonstrated partly by the invasion of men in Sappho's room in Ma Smith's house. Because the house belongs to his mother, Will Smith feels at liberty to enter Sappho's room without her permission. Sappho addresses his violation of her personal space: " 'I had no idea *you* were the fireman, Mr. Smith.…But you mustn't make my fire again' " (172, 174). Another occurrence is when Sappho tries to guard her personal space from villain John Langley, who believes he has the right to invade that space and her body. Asserting herself using combatant language, Sappho says, " 'Mr. Langley, your intrusion into my private apartment is unpardonable' " (318). For Sappho, female autonomy is realized in the power of dominion over personal space and body. Hopkins's attention to the intrusion of men in Sappho's female space reveals the nature of hegemonic oppression and its effect on female self-definition.

While Sappho's initial personal conversion from the New Orleans convent was short-lived because she suppressed her past, Sappho's volatile history, incited by her male assailant, returns her to the convent a second time. Hopkins's narrator makes a dreary statement about the raped black woman's temporary condition of purity in that her returned state of purity is short-lived:

> We may right a wrong, but we cannot restore our victim to his primeval state of happiness. Something is lost that can never be regained. The wages of sin is death. Innocent or guilty, the laws of nature are immutable. So with shoulders bent and misshapen with heavy burdens, the Negro plods along beating his cross—caring *the sins of others*. (332)

Though Sappho works through the traumatization of rape the first time at the convent, the stigma of degradation is still part of her moral fiber. If securing self-respect is important and possible for Sappho, she must move outside the characteristic boundaries of white "True Womanhood" and define herself differently. At the same time, what is important to understand here is that Sappho's and African American women's recovery requires a recovery or redemption of their history—the public and the private. As Chancy puts it, the initial efforts of a subject to "isolate herself from her past, to forget" are a "choice indicative of her need to recover memory, however painful that process might be" (176).

Essentially, Sappho must come to terms with her break or estrangement from her black identity and position that have been imposed upon her by others. Upon her move from the South, Sappho had left behind her identity as Mabelle, daughter of Monsieur Beaubean and "a quadroon woman" (258). When Sappho moves to Boston, she is literally a new woman—an independent woman. Because of her professional status as a stenographer, her charity work, and the suppression of her real name, family origins, and child, Sappho "performs an identity as a marriageable, single woman when, in fact, she is a mother and rape victim" (Brooks 102). Sappho's "hidden past is marked by Hopkins's description of Sappho's 'self-suppressed life' and her layered identity." For example, Hopkins distinguishes between what Dora perceives of Sappho in terms of her outward appearance (her beauty) and Dora's detection that Sappho is perhaps hiding something from her. Hopkins reveals further Dora's keen observation and curiosity about Sappho when Dora is "watching the changes on the mirror-like face of her friend whenever her attention was arrested by a new phenomenon" (Hopkins 115). Hopkins's attention to these details helps us to see Sappho as a split between the female Dora sees and the woman Sappho actually is. For Sappho, the "rupture" or split with her old identity and status as a virtuous woman is never resolved or regained in the new identity following her first departure from the New Orleans convent.

The conflict that Sappho must resolve is that of her identity and status as a rape victim and unwed mother, as opposed to the socially desirable status as marriageable woman, virtuous woman, and future wedded mother. The narrator explicitly shows that the matter of responsibility and the stereotype of licentious black women are identity stigmas carried over from slavery regarding the makeup of African American women. Questions of control and responsibility concerning female sexuality follow Sappho's first stay in the convent as a black rape victim. In Boston, Sappho struggles with both her identity and accountability as an African American woman and with whether she is in some ways to be blamed for her rape as seen earlier in the Sewing Circle. Growing up in a society that thought less of African Americans and considered them only as property, Sappho would likely have heard whites frequently speak poorly of blacks. Hopkins emphasizes the racist lack of remorse on the part of Sappho's rapist white uncle; even after sexually assaulting her, he places the responsibility of the rape on her and says Sappho " 'is no better than her mother or her grandmother. What does a woman of mixed blood, or any Negress, for that matter, know of virtue? It is my belief that they were a direct creation by God to be the pleasant companions of men of my race' " (261). Because of the rape and the consequent out-of-wedlock child, Sappho carried within herself the notion that she was a defiled and unworthy woman for marriage. Until meeting Mrs. Willis and the women in the Sewing Circle, Sappho believed that African American women, in some way, were responsible for the racial and sexual transgressions against them.

Hopkins demonstrates that the healing of the rupture in Sappho's identity as a virtuous black woman, mother, and partner for marriage must be realized in sites outside the dominant society's center, including black male culture that also dominates over black women. In the circle of the convent "sisters," Sappho regains control of her fractured identity as a nineteenth-century black woman, objecting to the dualistic thinking that she is an unworthy marriageable woman and resenting "to be the pleasant companion[s] of men" (261). In order to fulfill her goal, Hopkins, in her novel's preface, provides for reconciliation of black female virtue. Sappho is not ruined or destroyed like Grace Montfort. Instead, Sappho obtains a second chance at life in the North.

In her second retreat to the New Orleans convent for renewal and transformation, Sappho grows in new knowledge of her value and responsibility as a mother. From earlier feelings resulting from her uncle's rape, Sappho's "feeling of degradation had made her ashamed of the joys of motherhood, of pride of possession in her child. But all that feeling was swept away" (345). In her resolution to perform "her duty to guide and care" for her son, Sappho determines that "she would do her duty without shrinking" (345). Sappho's sense of her maternal obligation materializes when she accepts her role as mother to the child born as a result of her being raped. The approaching transformation for Sappho "is to break down the subject-object duality that keeps her a prisoner" (Anzaldua 102) and to begin to transform her female psyche. The process of claiming herself as a virtuous woman and mother emerges as Sappho understands how structures of domination work and the importance of finding female spaces in which to redeem and reclaim herself.

TRANSITORY SITES FOR FEMALE AUTONOMY

Unlike other female "spaces" found in sentimental novels, Hopkins's inversion of space is identified as "new places," sites of reviving and disengaging stereotypical identities as imposed by dominant ideology. Because the politics of location[5] determine women's positions and the ways they are able to access or reposition themselves in society, Hopkins suggests that "new spaces" are even more critical for black women redefining and recreating themselves as "True Women." The movement of the Transient Woman suggests that in these unbound "spaces" are particular philosophies that show the importance of black women moving freely in and out of dominant society's space. This movement is revolutionary in terms of African American women defining black womanhood outside of male dominance; it is one that Transient Women create outside the concept of "True Womanhood." Hopkins shows that healing the female psyche in women-centered sites is continuous and that the Transient Woman repeatedly seeks refuge when the female psyche needs replenishment. Depicting black women who challenge prevalent constructs of race and gender, Hopkins creates transitory sites from which African American women gain sustenance and autonomy through female-centered sites and interactions.

4

AT THE CROSSROADS OF BLACK FEMALE AUTONOMY, OR DIGRESSION AS RESISTANCE IN *QUICKSAND* AND *THE STREET*

Yet when we few remain in that "other" space, we are often too isolated, too alone. We die there, too. Those of us who live, who "make it," passionately holding on to aspects of that "down-home" life we do not intend to lose while simultaneously seeking new knowledge and experience, invent spaces of radical openness. Without such spaces we would not survive. Our living depends on our ability to conceptualize alternatives, often improvised. Theorizing about this experience aesthetically and critically is an agenda for radical cultural practice.

—bell hooks[1]

This third space displaces the histories that constitute it, and sets up new structures of authority, new political initiatives, which are inadequately understood through received wisdom.

—Homi K. Bhabha[2]

bell hooks, in "The Politics of Radical Black Subjectivity," makes a critical claim on the opposition and the response of the oppressed once resistance is actualized. She asserts that opposing the oppressor is never enough. In the process toward subjectivity when one arrives at an understanding of "how structures of domination work" (15), one must continue the progression of self-development to make real the revolution that took place in the moment of "rage and resentment." hooks argues, "In that vacant space after one has resisted there is still the necessity

to become—to make oneself anew" (*Yearning* 15). This assertion implies that the oppressed or the marginalized, in their
move to selfhood, must continue the course of action for subjectivity. Resistance demands more than the fleeting moment
of rebellion; it requires of developing subjects the revisionist
work on the psyche to remain persistent in their liberatory
efforts. At the heart of this resistance are African American
women whose marginalized positions have prompted them to
resist their existence on the border of hegemonic order. To
change their conditions, black women have used their fictional
works as a place to focus on empowering black women by moving them from locations that place them on the edge of society
to ones that place them in the center of dominant discourse.
Authors Nella Larsen and Ann Petry address the issue of black
female marginal existence and force a discussion of locations in
which African American women can realize black female transformation and possibilities for change. These locations for black
female subjectivity resist boundaries. As Chancy notes,

> It is in exile that such awareness of the limitations imposed upon
> the [black woman's psyche] becomes much clearer; for "out
> there" women have the opportunity to speak out against their
> marginalization in a culture which is not theirs. (5)

Addressing the issue of safe space, Chancy points out that, for
black women, being located in sites outside the hegemony can
be good. To begin a radical change, it is necessary for black
women to seek safe and separate spaces. However, the other
part of this discussion is the significance of why developing subjects cannot remain in that " 'other space' "; it is the reality, as
hooks makes clear, that they can "die there" (*Yearning* 148).
    As part of the discussion on safe space, this chapter focuses
on Larsen's *Quicksand* (1928) and Petry's *The Street* (1946) as
narratives of enslavement and examines black female characters
who do not move to other locations outside the hegemony,
resulting in disastrous consequences for them. A problem for
Helga Crane and Lutie Johnson is the action they take after
experiencing hegemonic practices that prevent black female
autonomy. Though Helga and Lutie initially move from places

that hinder change, they do not complete female transformation when they do not move to Third Space or women-centered locations. The disrupted process is seen when they retreat from the point of self-realization by remaining in spaces that deter autonomy.

This chapter examines "Flight," the fourth phase of the Transient Woman. Specifically, the chapter shows "Flight" or "Digression" as an essential component in the process toward female transformation. This examination addresses why it is necessary for Helga and Lutie to move away from dominant forces and what prevents Helga and Lutie from moving to Third Space or women-centered locations. Moreover, the examination answers these questions: In what sense does safe space or location make a difference in articulating subjectivity? How important is it and how should space and its supposed effects for African American women be understood differently from other groups?

THIRD SPACE FOR BLACK FEMALE SUBJECTIVITY

The importance of Third Space, as a postcolonial construct, conceptualizes the necessity and locality in which Helga and Lutie have greater possibilities for black female expression and personal change. Defined by Bhabha as "in-between" spaces, in this place, cultural meaning and value are negotiated. It is a location from which a group, through its displacement, opens new spaces to articulate difference and form new strategies for self-representation. The moment individuals or groups become aware of their differences is the time to deliberate on the course of action for subjectivity. It is precisely in a secured location, as Bhabha asserts, that it

> provide[s] the terrain for elaborating strategies of selfhood—singular or communal—that initiate new signs of identity, and innovative sites of collaboration, and contestation, in the act of defining the idea of society itself. (*Location* 1–2)

Away from the gaze of the "master," Helga and Lutie, in Third Space or a women-centered site, can set the parameters by which they can define themselves and provide for themselves the tools necessary to exist autonomously within the dominant culture's space without the risk of "dying there" as hooks maintains.

My argument for moving to safe spaces for resistance and redefinition differs from Farah Jasmine Griffin's and demonstrates that these strategies are required for recovering and reconstructing the female self before moving to the center of dominant discourse. Griffin believes that safe spaces are at most resistant acts. She argues, "At their most reactionary, they are potentially provincial spaces which do not encourage resistance but instead create complacent subjects whose only aim is to exist with the confines of power that oppress them" (9). My view differs from Griffin's assessment that marginalized women who move to new spaces for resistance and renewal make complacent subjects. Here, in this study, I emphasize that the marginalization and silence that oppresses and exploits black women "is broken and replaced with particularly feminist visions of the plausibility and possibility of also breaking the cycle," as Chancy emphasizes, "of that oppression and its diverse manifestations" (xxi). Using women-centered spaces for resistance is a radical act that supports the history of black women as revolutionized visionaries in breaking from continued hegemonic oppression.

Separate and safe space, as a transitory site, is imperative for Helga and Lutie to progress to black female selfhood. Given that Helga is viewed and sexualized as an "exotic peacock" and Lutie is conceived by men and Mrs. Hedges as a sexual object willing to trade herself for survival, these depictions of black women demonstrate the racial pejoratives displayed in mainstream society. Because of the controlled negative images that continue to follow African American women, it is nearly impossible for Larsen's and Johnson's heroines to make significant change to their material conditions within hegemonic locations. Larsen's and Johnson's seeming intent, as black female novelists, is to provide choices for their female characters in changing how they see themselves and their positions as black women and that a transformation to both must begin and materialize first in sites away from the dominant forces. Possible changes to Helga's female self are countered in New York and Denmark. Similarly, actualizing subjectivity is unfeasible for Lutie while existing on 116th Street in Harlem. Thus, the need for and the construction of separate space away from oppressive forces open possibilities for change in the development of selfhood and a new black female consciousness—a consciousness different from the model of "True Womanhood."[3] In this location the black female psyche[4] can be restored in a neutral space that is not empowered by white ideological values and superiority.

Noting the significant effect of location is Carla L. Peterson, who supports separate space for African American women. In her study of nineteenth-century African American women speakers and writers, she looks at the likelihood of a separate location for black women resistance and explains,

> My study asks whether it is possible to imagine a scenario whereby the incarcerated could escape, and perhaps even return, the gaze of their wardens; undo the dominant culture's definitions of such binary oppositions as order/disorder, normal/abnormal, harmless/dangerous; break down those boundaries separating the one from the Other; and in the process create a space that they could call home. (8)

The idea of constructing new black female identities is possible and best understood in finding a separate space that allows transformation to occur. Although Peterson uses the term "home" loosely in connection with separate space, in my study, "home" does not equate with "permanency." In Third Space, "home" is a temporary site for transformation and renewal.

By using Third Space as a place of resistance and restoration of the female psyche for African American women, Helga and Lutie can defy the continuation of Otherness. Domination is certain in any social order. However, it is unlikely to have much force, if any, in a space where the oppressed articulate their existence freely. "This realm of relatively safe discourse, however narrow is a necessary condition for Black women's resistance" (100–101). Collins explains, "These spaces are not only safe—they form prime locations for resisting objectification as the Other" (101). In this secure space, African American women are free to define and articulate their selves by their own standards.

A separate black female space for resisting hegemonic practices is necessary for Larsen's and Johnson's female characters within their own black communities. "African American men and black communities have…perpetuated racist, sexist, elitist, and homophobic ideologies" (Collins 101) that pressure African American women to act and perform in certain ways. For example, Zora Neale Hurston's literary skills were censured by African American male writers during and after the Harlem Renaissance. Some viewed her narrative strategy of using black dialect as offensive and not in step with the "New Negro." "Alain Locke, wrote…that Hurston's *Their Eyes* was simply out of step with the more serious trends of the times…Richard Wright excoriated *Their Eyes* as a novel that did for literature what the minstrel shows did for theater, that is make white folks laugh" (Washington viii). Under the race umbrella that dictated acceptable African American writing, Hurston was censored in writing about issues and using language that did not promote the "New Negro"[5] in the early 1930s. Likewise, "race" men dictated black female sexual mores and behavior, which in effect prevented Hurston from writing sufficiently about black female sexuality. Regrettably, Harlem Renaissance black male writers did not understand and accept Hurston's use of the black vernacular and her gender-specific contributions to African American literature.

That black communities ostracize African American women who do not meet standards set by male ideology points to black women's need to move from such communities. Consider, for example, Morrison's *Sula*. Sula goes against the sexual norms set by black communities. Snubbed by the men and women in the Bottom for her peculiarity, Sula is marked as a shameless black woman for her choice in sexual partners. The narrator reports,

> But it was the men who gave her the final *label* (*emphasis added*), who fingerprinted her for all time. They were the ones who said she was guilty of the forgivable thing—the thing for which there was no understanding, no excuse, no compassion. . . . They said that Sula slept with white men. . . . All minds were closed to her when that word was passed around. It made the old women draw their lips together; made small children look away from her in shame; made young men fantasize elaborate torture for her—just to get the saliva back in their mouths when they saw her. (Morrison 112–113)

Because of Sula's actions, including placing her grandmother Eva in a retirement home and having an affair with her best friend's husband, she is judged to be the worst of women. Not having any real evidence that points to Sula sleeping with white men, the black community nevertheless judges her as immoral and abnormal.

As the men in the Bottom are the fundamental holders of power, sexual standards for black men are judged differently. The narrator informs us that the same men who judge Sula unfairly are the men who "lie in the beds of white women. Yet the black men [are] unwilling to accept Sula stepping out from the race.... They insist that all unions between white men and black women be rape; for a black woman to be willing [wa]s literally unthinkable" (113). Because of such views and double standards set by black men and the black community, Sula had departed earlier from the Bottom to seek a place away from the judgment of the black social order.

As separate spaces and places are important to African American women's survival, these safe places must include black female support. In such spaces, African American women find, through female relationships, spiritual sustenance. When black women move away from oppression, for survival and resistance, for recuperation, and for self-definition and autonomy, safe spaces become critically essential. An example of female spiritual sustenance is portrayed in the description Morrison gives of Nel and Sula's relationship. Morrison writes that Nel and Sula "found relief" through their relationship: "They found in each other's eyes the intimacy they were looking for" (52). Sula and Nel's intimacy solidifies their commonality to find who they are in a system that devalues their realities as black females.

How do female bonds and separate space in a woman-centered location realize black women's resistance and self-actualization? In these spaces, "What power do [black women] have to effect change in societies which advocate for [their] subordination?" (Chancy 13). The transformation from Other to subject takes place in spaces that are not influenced by white and patriarchal societies. It is reasonable that if women, as marginalized beings, are to realize selfhood and what Lorde asserts is an "interdependency between women...(111), then female connectiveness allows female self-invention. Lorde illuminates female nurturance as redemptive and argues that "it is within that knowledge of women's redeeming power that [women's] real power is rediscovered" (111). In the affirmation of women-centeredness as a source of female knowledge and power, Lorde's assertion alludes to places outside male dominion.

For Larsen's and Petry's heroines, a women-centered location offers safe places for nurturance, renewal, and reconfirmation of the black female self. What is evident in female locations is the foundation it provides for black women "to counter their multiple points of oppression and generate their own sense of self as they move" in and out of the hegemony's center (Chancy 14). What might be considered self-isolation or refutation becomes the means of self-liberation. The need to migrate to black female space becomes increasingly clear in the situations of Helga Crane in *Quicksand* and Lutie Johnson in *The Street*.

The interconnections of viable safe spaces and female relationships in sustaining female subjectivity are evidenced in the literature of African American writers. Particularly in showing how female support helps brace black women as a means of survival. For example, in safe female spaces, Celie, in Alice Walker's *The Color Purple*, develops self-awareness and self-confidence. In the company of black women like herself, Celie is able to understand her position as a black woman and critically learns from other black women how to endure within male order. The circle of women becomes for Celie the female community as conceptualized in the Transient Woman's Third Space to resist objectification. Celie writes in a letter, " 'Now that my eyes opening,...Still, it is like Shug say, You have to git man off your eyeball, before you can see anything' " (Walker 197). Celie realizes that hegemonic power is strong or evident only if she allows it; and it is through female connections that she can prevail. In regard to Celie's female circle and "interactions with these self-confident women," Michael Awkward contends,

> From her friendship...and Celie begins to develop not only a higher self-regard, but also a sense of the benefits of community. These women come to represent for Celie "present" audiences to

whom she can speak about the burdens of her life and from whom, unlike her absent Reader, she receives immediate and beneficial response. (153)

Awkward's observation demonstrates that female interconnections for Helga and Lutie are part of the survival mechanisms that might have prevented their annihilation by the end of the story. Within female spheres and friendships, black women can relate like experiences and devise strategies against female oppression and extinction.

Disruption of Black Female Consciousness

Given that black female transformation can be realized through the five stages of the Transient Woman, there are instances when the process toward female renewal and autonomy is disrupted by a false sense of consciousness. Such interruptions occur when the female believes she is knowledgeable and equipped to interrelate with the hegemony. In *The Street*, Lutie's undeveloped female confidence is tested when she pretends she is not looking for the same things as the other women who come to Junto's bar. While the "young women had an urgent hunger for companionship," Lutie thinks "she wasn't going to Junto to pick up a man" (144). Lutie believes she is "street wise" and will not fall prey to men who snare women as a game. Unluckily, Lutie's visit to the bar guides her to the man who leads her to her bad end.

Lutie's sense of female consciousness has not been fully tested; even more importantly, it has not been infused with female energy from a community of African American women. Individual effort to change the status of black women's peripheral existence yields little in the advancement of African American women as a whole. It must be a communal endeavor, as Lorde insists:

When Black women in this country come together to examine [their] sources of strength and support, and to recognize our common social, cultural, emotional, and political interests, it is a development which can only contribute to the power of the Black community as a whole. It can certainly never diminish it. For it is through the coming together of *self-actualized individuals*...that any real advances can be made. (46 *emphasis added*)

The approach to female reform as understood here shows that the Transient Woman is positioned for a full transformation if it is through a shared effort with a black female spiritual connection.

Indeed, African American women who interrupt the steps to black female consciousness and do not shift to women-centered locations or Third Space are certain to face serious consequences. Larsen and Petry present female characters who experience certain psychological deaths when they remain in sites that maintain subjugation. Though both Helga and Lutie move through the first three stages of the Transient Woman, they fall short of completing the process when they continue to exist and engage with hegemony. The works illustrate the danger in lingering within the circle of oppression without a departure to Third Space or women-centered locations for renewal or change. As cultural signs and values draw their meaning from hegemony, how might it be possible for black women to exert agency in making new meaning of their lives if they remain in the precise places that define them as Other? Because of their differences and objectification, African American women must move outside the dominant's space—a space in which they are invisible—to reevaluate and reassess their social positions.

This necessary shift from hegemonic space is revealed in *Quicksand* and *The Street*, wherein the female protagonists experience distressing endings. Each coming from different social and economic backgrounds, their fates are similar in trying to survive. Survival in the domain of hegemonic power includes arranging time and place to refurbish the female psyche to face the constant battle within specific race, gender, and cultural politics. While Helga and Lutie are both women arriving at female knowledge in the stories, what is clear in both novels is that they do not grasp that after coming into awareness of how hegemony works, they must move temporarily from their existing space and find renewal within a community of women. hooks writes that "after one has resisted there is still the necessity to become—to make oneself anew" (*Yearning* 15). To remain in hegemonic space and fight alone is a fruitless battle for Helga and Lutie. Only after they create an oppositional stance in unison with struggling women like themselves can Helga and Lutie realize complete black female transformation. Helga and Lutie must evolve to a female realm for change, but in their digression to remain in oppositional space, they fail to discover this lesson.

Possessing new female knowledge and failing to respond to the workings of male dominance, at the end of *Quicksand*, Helga experiences a psychosomatic death. After years of trying to find her place in black and white societies and after moves to and from geographical locales, Helga succumbs to her marginalized position as a black woman and wastes away as wife of the "countrified" Rev. Pleasant Green of rural Alabama. Helga, the once-sophisticated woman, now "exists only as a fading illusion in the memories, fantasies, and dreams of a despondent and debilitated wife" (Tate 119). She gives up her upper-middle class and accepts the "womenfolks'" image of herself as "Pore Mis' Green" (Larsen 116) and is locked into helplessness. As Larsen demonstrates by the end, Helga endures a literal and symbolic death due to her inertia to act upon her "erotic" knowledge. She gives up herself and yields to "the dinginess of her physical surroundings (poverty), the lack of intellectual stimulation,…the continual strain of childbearing," and the lack of female companionship, "drawing her into the quicksand from which she had been trying to escape" (Christian, *Black Women Novelists* 52–53).

In the beginning of the story, Larsen portrays a more confident and aggressive woman who is nothing like the dejected female at the end. She is characterized as "a sensuous mulatta of questionable parentage who is repulsed by the drab puritanism of middle-class Negro society" (*Black Women Novelists* 48). Finding refuge in her personal space after "insulting remarks" by "that holy white man" to the students and faculty at Naxos (2), Helga tries to dismiss the "surg[ing]…hot anger and seething resentment" (3) she has for white ideology and her "overpowering desire for action of some sort" (4). Helga, an unconventional woman by the 1930s standards, is not afraid to voice her differences on how middle-class intellectuals perform in a black-operated school under white tutelage.

However Helga is cognizant of the time to speak against white double standards and the moment to let go and wait for a better time. Helga's awareness of hegemonic power is evident in her teaching students to fight against oppression and in "her own earnest endeavor to inculcate knowledge into her indifferent classes" at Naxos (4). With white benefactors like the speaker at the early morning session, Helga understands that the space within Naxos, a black community, is programmed in the ideology of the dominant power they try to escape. She thinks,

> This great community…was no longer a school. It had grown into a machine. It was now a show place in the black belt, exemplification of the white man's magnanimity, refutation of the black man's inefficiency. Life had died out of it. It was, [she] decided, now only a big knife with cruelly sharp edges ruthlessly cutting all to a pattern, the white-man's pattern. Teachers as well as students were subjected to the paring process, for it tolerated no innovations, no individualisms. Ideas it rejected, and looked with open hostility on one and all who had the temerity to offer suggestion or ever so mildly express a disapproval. Enthusiasm, spontaneity, if not actually suppressed were at least openly regretted as unladylike or ungentlemanly qualities. The place was smug and fat with self-satisfaction. (4)

As Christian points out, Helga "sees the lie behind this distinguished Negro school" (49). Helga recognizes that even in black communities, African Americans are conditioned to act according to white standards and white approval. Like racially mixed females molded to white standards of past Quadroon balls to be bought, Naxos is bought or commodified by white sponsorships, its mission being to turn out black students in the "white man's pattern" (4).

In spite of the "trivial hypocrisies" and "fighting the devil" (5), Helga tries to stay on at Naxos to change the mind-set of the students. She has struggled within her own power to provide support and to "befriend those happy singing children, whose charm and distinctiveness the school was so surely ready to destroy" (5). After almost two years teaching at Naxos,

Helga's zest for teaching gives out. She thinks about her time at Naxos, which operates under oppressive structures, and how it has affected her way of thinking:

> Helga, on the other hand, had never quite achieved the unmistakable Naxos mold, would never achieve it, in spite of much trying. She could neither conform, nor be happy in her unconformity. This she saw clearly now, and with cold anger at all the past futile effort. What a waste! How pathetically she had struggled in those first months and with what small success. (7)

Helga understands that for her to exist in a place where conventionality of thought is outside herself, she must move to a space of resistance that allows for what hooks describes as a "location of radical openness and possibility" (*Yearning* 153). Such self-reflection removes Helga from places that deter her journey to female determination and self-autonomy and suggests possibility of self-growth on Helga's part.

Collins writes that "black women's journey often involves the 'transformation of silence into language and action'" (113). Having been reserved at Naxos, Helga makes up her mind to leave when she tells her teacher-friend Margaret that "she cannot stand another minute of teaching at Naxos and must leave immediately" (Christian, *Black Women Novelists* 50). As a friend, Margaret is troubled by Helga's possible struggle in trying to make it as a black woman and professional outside Naxos. Helga retorts, "Thanks a thousand times, Margaret. I'm really awfully grateful, but—you see it's like this, I'm not going to be late to my class. I'm not going to be there at all" (13). Such a reply is from a woman of female consciousness who understands that she cannot fight the system without giving up herself. hooks points out that when a people "no longer have the space to construct homeplace, [they] cannot build a meaningful community of resistance (*Yearning* 47)." Helga does depart from Naxos, and the remainder of the story focuses on Helga traveling to places seemingly in search of an elusive something that will fulfill her.

Larsen's portrayal of Helga's feelings and resolve to move from oppressive places points metaphorically to the Transient Woman's epiphany when she moves from a hegemonic location to Third Space. After disillusionment with the black community at Naxos, Helga "wishe[d] it was vacation, so that she might get away for a *time*" from the continual oppression of hegemony (*emphasis added*) (3). In Helga's mind, the "vacation" time away is only temporary, but it suggests her move or journey to renew:

> At last she *stirred*, uncertainly, but with an overpowering desire for action of some sort. A second she hesitated, then rose abruptly and pressed the electric switch with determined firmness, flooding suddenly the shadowy with a white glare of light. (*emphasis added*) (4)

Even before this moment, Helga has arrived at black female consciousness. With her "stir[ring]," Helga is cognizant of the power of hegemony and understands the point at which she must move herself away from its ideology. She understands that she must act before she is drawn into the "quicksand" of hegemonic difference.

The imagery of Helga's stalwartness with the "electric switch" suggests Helga's female knowledge and the point that she knows she cannot linger in places that subjugate her and others to the dictates of the oppressor. The charged switch, in this situation, represents for Helga the "erotic" that Lorde identifies as the power or energy within women to pursue change within their lives. Lorde emphasizes that

> when we begin to live...in touch with the power of the erotic within ourselves, and allowing that power to inform and *illuminate* our actions...then we begin to be responsible to ourselves..., we begin to give up, of necessity, being satisfied with suffering and self-negation, and...Our acts against oppression become integral with self, motivated and empowered from within. (*emphasis added*) (58)

In touch with her erotic, Helga relies on her female knowledge or consciousness to move out and away from oppression. As this is a conscious choice on the part of the Transient Woman, she does so unreservedly to save herself from the sure failure that would entail her remaining in places that repress. In the "vacation" time that Helga had thought of earlier, she would be forced to come to terms with who she is as a black woman, rather than conforming to what she is not, when subject to the standards of the "white man's pattern" (Larsen 4).

Though she begins to gain self-awareness, Helga, a learned, articulate, and cultured woman, comes to a tragic end because she does not know how to deal with an oppressive society. She is not equipped to move beyond the problems black women face day to day since she has not moved to a safe location to regroup and learn new resistance tactics. Reinventing or renewing the self is a process. The progression, as hooks asserts,

> emerges as one comes to understand how structures of domination work in one's life, as one develops critical thinking and critical consciousness, as one invents new, alternative habits of being, and resists from that marginal space of difference inwardly defined. (*Yearning* 15)

Though hooks names the space of difference as marginal, it is to Third Space and "Beyond" that Helga needs to transition in order to locate and use female tools to resist. Even as Helga understood hegemonic practices of excluding and oppressing women, she failed to remain true to her self and to continue in the state of female consciousness. If Helga had reacted and responded in the same way as she did to the Naxos system, she may have survived, before her final decline and destruction when she returns to the rural South.

Similarly, Lutie Johnson's ending in *The Street* is as tragic as Helga's psychosomatic death. Lutie's death is also a self-inflicted emotional and mental death. The ending paragraph of Petry's novel reports the outcome of Lutie's misdirection. Running away from a gruesome scene after murdering Boots Smith, Lutie is moving to another place to find a beginning. Moving and traveling to new places is not new to Lutie. Earlier, she had moved to Jamaica NY with her husband, Jim, to find a better place in life. After discovering Jim's extramarital affair, she moves again. With her son Bub, Lutie moves to Harlem to find safe sanctuary. However, in the fleeting moment while traveling to Chicago after the murder and leaving her eight-year-old son to fend for himself, Lutie is reminded of her position as a black woman in America. She remembers her teacher's comments on cultivating black girls like herself:

> Once again she could hear the flat, exasperated voice of the teacher as she looked at the circles Lutie had produced. "Really," she said, "I don't know why they have us bother to teach your people to write." The circles showed up plainly on the dusty surface. The woman's statement was correct, she thought. What possible good has it done to teach people like me to write? (Petry 435–436)

This passage reflects the end for Lutie. She gives in to the hegemonic conception of the ill-wasted effort and time in teaching allegedly unteachable African Americans. In contrast to the beginning and middle of the novel, where Petry portrays an intelligent, strong-willed African American female, the end of the story has Lutie fall prey to the hegemonic design for the marginalized—a trapped life on the margins of white society.

Like Helga, Lutie realizes the third phase of the Transient Woman in coming to know of how the hegemony dominates and oppresses. Leaving Jamaica and taking a position as maid to the Chandlers, Lutie learns quickly the difference between her life as a black woman and the white Mrs. Chandler's. The first time Lutie meets her new white employer, she "was thinking too hard" about their differences as women (36). Everything Mrs. Chandler wears speaks of value and class. Lutie compares herself and feels that "what she's got on makes everything I'm wearing look cheap" (36). In Lutie's mind, Mrs. Chandler as a white woman has been given a better life—a life with privileges and wealth.

As Lutie understands, race and gender control how others see her. In spite of how she conducts herself and relates with Mrs. Chandler, Lutie is associated with the controlling images of African American women and identified as a sexual object. She overhears the exchanges between Mrs. Chandler and her white female friends. They warn Mrs. Chandler of the danger she is in by having an attractive black female in her home: " 'But I wouldn't have any good-looking colored wench in my house. Not with John. You know they's always making passes at men.

Especially white men'" (40–41). Lutie "wonder[s] why they all had the idea that colored girls were whores" and sees that she is invisible in their world (41). Outside the circle of hegemony definition, Lutie must locate female self-definition in a realm that allows for full and whole development as a woman.

Regardless of how hard she tries to show that black women are not lascivious and mindless, as structures of domination imagines them, Lutie realizes that this dominant society will not accept her. Lutie observes the barriers that the hegemony uses to keep black women on the edge of society. The difference in how the dominant society's members treat her when she is in their "center" becomes increasingly clear when she interfaces with hegemony social order. Lutie notes,

> It was, she discovered slowly, a very strange world that she had entered. With an entirely different set of values. It made her feel that she was looking through a hole in a wall at some enchanted garden. She could see, she could hear, she spoke the language of the people in the garden, but she couldn't get past the wall. The figures on the other side of it loomed up life-size and they could see her, but there was this wall in between which pre-vented them from mingling on an equal footing. The people on the other side of the wall knew less about her than she knew about them.
>
> She decided it wasn't just because she was a maid; it was because she was colored. (41)

The position in which the hegemonic order places her is one that preempts her and her family's efforts at a better life. Despite how refined she thinks she is and her use of the master's lan-guage, the hegemony defines her differently and as hierar-chically inferior.

Race and gender become even more distressing for Lutie when she learns that the white domestic male workers are better treated than she is. Class does not come into view for white male domestic workers in the Chandler's household. While Lutie is viewed as different without access to white privilege and respect, she observes that the white male landscaper is dis-cerned as less threatening and treated as an equal. "Even the man who mowed the lawn and washed the windows and weeded the garden didn't move behind a wall that effectively and automatically placed him in some previously prepared classification" (41). When Mrs. Chandler drives him to the train station after a day's work, Lutie sees that he is treated like an old friend and weekend guest. Mrs. Chandler extends and shakes his hand when he gets out the car. However, when Mrs. Chandler is in public view, she treats Lutie like a maid and the "wall" suddenly appears even moments after they acted as equals in talking "about some story being played up in the newspapers, about clothes or some moving picture" (51).

Equipped with the knowledge of how hegemony works, Lutie is responsible for her ultimate fall and relegation to the margins. Part of Lutie's problem stems from her acceptance of values of the dominant culture. Working for the white Chandlers, "she absorbed some of the same spirit," believing that the American Dream was possible for her as an African American woman (43). Like Helga in *Quicksand*, Lutie is not equipped and prepared to fend off white values that distort her thinking.

Bernard W. Bell comments on Lutie's predicament: "The irony is that Lutie sees, yet fails to act on, the price that the Chandlers pay in spiritual and personal alienation for their material success" (108). The myth of the American Dream keeps Lutie going when she wants to give up. When she is tired of working and attending night school, Lutie thinks of the Chandlers and the opportunities they had to seek their dreams: "Every time it seemed as though she couldn't possibly summon the energy to go on with the course, she would remind herself of all the people who had got somewhere in spite of the odds against them. She would think of the Chandlers and their young friends" (Petry 55). Lutie is out of touch with black reality in comparing herself to the whites with whom she comes in contact.

Instead of seeing how the system works to suppress black women like herself and instead of falling back on the support of black women's community, Lutie loses a part of her black female knowledge when she believes that entering white society is the only avenue in escaping the margins of white society. Williams contends that the "cultural domination of blacks by whites means that the black self is placed at a distance even from itself" (62).

Lutie, in this case, is not able to visualize herself as anything different from whites when justifying her trust in the white way of living.

In Lutie's quest for economic freedom, she overlooks her social reality as a working-class black woman and falls into the trap of believing in the possibility of the American Dream and "experiences it failures" (Pettis 25). "Myths are not rational," writes James O. Robertson in *American Myth, American Reality,* "at least in the sense that they are not controlled by what we believe to be logic. They are sometimes based on faith, on belief rather than reason, on ideals rather than realities" (qtd. by Bell 106). In this situation, the myth of the American Dream is a negative response to Lutie's dilemma as black and female. Lutie's acquired black female knowledge is subjugated in the dreams that are constructed for those who have power over those like her on the margins. Unfortunate for Lutie, who even adapts Benjamin Franklin's ideals of hard work, she realizes too late that no amount of hard work or savings would move her from 116th Street. "Petry's use of dramatic irony—that the model of the self-made man that Benjamin Franklin represents does not [and] was never intended to include women or black men" (Pryse, "Pattern" 118). In the end and after killing a man who dupes her, Lutie abandons her son to the myth that the system "kills" black men. She is a fugitive—a woman running for her life, one who does not have a place to which to run.

Relative to the myth of American Dream, both authors demonstrate that black female realization is understood outside sites that hinder black women's development. Pettis points out that many African American women writers have addressed the "schism that occurs when blacks—particularly women—ignore the politics (and lessons) of race, class, and gender and blindly subscribe to the American Dream" (115). Larsen observes places for African Americans such as Naxos that are white influenced and are adverse to black's whole advancement. After coming to the knowledge of how hegemony functions to destroy black female consciousness, African American women must be prepared to move from such places in order to complete female transformation in a place that nurtures and revitalizes black female spirits. The next section describes the events that lead to Helga Crane's and Lutie Johnson's downfall and argues that their survival depends upon departure from hegemony order and their pursuance of female bonding.

Black Female Support for Survival

In view of the disruption in the process toward female consciousness with the incidents that lead to their protagonists' final ends, Larsen and Petry offer more in their narratives that point to the female protagonists' breakdowns. Though Helga Crane in *Quicksand* dies from the constraints of marriage and multiple births and Lutie Johnson in *The Street* gives up from broken dreams and promises, their demise is also brought on by the lack of black female support. Helga is surrounded by others and sometimes other females, but her actual time spent in black female companionship is limited. She has only a professional connection with fellow teacher Margaret, whom she sometimes thinks of as an unequal or as someone who is not like her. To have a meaningful relationship with Margaret, Helga must think of her as equivalent to her and not condescendingly as she does when she thinks how outrageous Margaret is in straightening her "nice live crinkly hair…into a dead straight greasy, ugly mass" (Larsen 14). As Christian notes, this is a response from someone light-skinned with abundant "curly blue-black hair" and who has "earned her whatever respectability she enjoyed at Naxos" (*Black Women Novelists* 50).

Similarly, Helga's relationship with Anne Grey is one of convenience and not for female friendship. Because Helga lives in Anne's home, she feels mostly an obligation to be cordial rather than any genuine "sisterly" attitude toward Anne. She acts and exists with Anne out of a guilty conscience "so she wanted to be particularly nice to Anne, who had been kind to her when first she came to New York, a forlorn friendless creature" (56). Helga does not seek or want a relationship with Anne. In fact, she detests Anne and makes every effort to be out of Anne's space: "The gentle Anne distressed her. Perhaps because Anne was obsessed by the race problem and fed her obsession" (48). The desire to move away from Anne becomes more determined after a disagreement with Anne over Audrey Denney, whom Anne views as " 'the disgusting creature!' " (60). Instead of trying to discuss and understand why Anne feels this way, Helga avoids Anne, since "she didn't want to quarrel with Anne, not now, when she had that guilty feeling about leaving her" (61). Helga, in some ways, is narcissistic and uses others for her selfish means. True relationships are built on trust, respect, and sharing; Helga is unable to have this bond with any woman.

Likewise, Helga's relationship with the women in the rural community where she ultimately lives is one in which Helga sees them as indifferent and below her. As in earlier times when Helga finds something interesting or new after a period of dislike or dissatisfaction, she projects that she is sincere in her feelings. However, Helga seemingly resorts to the same white missionaries' intent as in the example of Naxos to "civilize." The narrator reveals,

> Eagerly she accepted everything, even that bleak air of poverty which in some curious way, regards itself as virtuous, for no other reason than that it is poor....She meant to subdue the cleanly scrubbed ugliness of her own surroundings to soft inoffensive beauty, and to help the women to do likewise....She visualized herself instructing the children, who seemed most of the time to run wild, in ways of gentler deportment.
>
> She went about to try to interest the women in what she considered more appropriate clothing and in inexpensive ways of improving their homes according to her ideas of beauty. (emphasis added) (119)

In this instance, Helga believes and feels that it is her duty to cultivate and advance the women according to her standards. Clearly, there is a patronizing relationship on the part of Helga with the women. If Helga was sincere in building female relations or friendships, she would do so without feeling the need to help them advance from their "countrified" way of living to the conduct of the middle class to which she is accustomed.

Also, Lutie, in *The Street*, lacks female relationships for support. Though the story does not focus on female relationships, Petry draws out the conclusion that female relationships are necessary for healthy and holistic black female survival. Had Lutie nurtured female relationships with the women on 116th Street, perhaps she and Bub might have survived their dismal environment. Bub might not have fallen under the influence of Jones and been on the streets when Lutie was working. Instead he might have been under the "watchful eye" and care of Mrs. Hedges and Min. If Lutie had female support, she would have turned to female friendships for help instead of relying on male power as in the corrupt white lawyer and band leader. Perhaps, Petry's intent is to show that black women are survivors despite the obstacles they face daily, including the racialized myths. Particularly interesting is how Petry sets up her female characters to counteract the stereotypes inflicted on black women. Because she arranges the women in the story with "particular physical characteristics that match specific stereotypes and then proceeds to show how they are not quite what they seem...she both adheres to and deviates from the standard images" used, for example, with the tragic mulatta figure who is "cut off from any community" (*Black Women Novelists* 65).

However, the most obvious female relationship and the closest that Lutie has in the story is the one with her grandmother. Though the novel does not provide instances of dialogue between Lutie and Granny, it shows how Granny's values directly impact Lutie's decisive moments. Because Granny is old and out of touch with modern ways of thinking, Lutie dismisses Granny's ideas about men as foolish warnings. For example, at a time when Lutie should use Granny's wisdom about being alone with strange men, Lutie dismisses Granny's early warnings of danger when she finds herself dangerously alone with Super Jones. Instinctively, Lutie feels Jones's sexual longing for her and "even while she thought it, the hot, choking awfulness of his desire for her," she rejects the sense of danger and believes it is not "possible to read people's minds" and that Jones is not feeling what her intuition and Granny warn her about (Petry 93). Lutie considers,

> Now the Super was probably not even thinking about her when he was standing there like that....She was as bad as Granny. Which just went on to prove you couldn't be brought up by

someone like Granny without absorbing a lot of nonsense that would spring at you out of nowhere....All those tales about things that people sensed before they actually happened....And Granny had them all at the tip of her tongue. (Petry 15–16)

Lutie mistakenly views Granny's years of experience as absurd. A problem for Lutie is her lack of awareness and her failure to accept the power of female influence.

Female bonding is useful and essential in building confidence for black women's survival. The shared recognition of the threats to black women is paramount for their continued existence. Within and through black female connection, women avoid self-annihilation. Outside and away from strong black female bonding, Lutie unreasonably goes against better judgment and her own intuition that points to jeopardy. Lutie thinks,

There was no explaining away the instinctive, immediate fear she had felt when she first saw the Super. Granny would have said, "Nothin' but evil, child...." She didn't believe things like that and yet, looking at his tall, gaunt figure going down that last flight of stairs ahead of her, she half-expected to see horns sprouting from behind his ears. (20)

Had Lutie regarded Granny's wisdom in paying attention to her intuitive feelings, she might not have moved to the apartment with Jones, which eventually leads to her and Bub losing hold of their lives.

As a comment on why novelists Larsen and Petry offer heroines without female support and nurturance, Christian offers an interesting point why Petry's, unlike other black women writers', female heroine is cut off from female companionship—from within "the church, a tight circle of friends, or the family" (*Black Women Novelists* 64). Christian comments, "In this sense, Petry stays close to the tendency of many protest writers to see black culture, as nonfunctional. Perhaps that is because Petry's purpose in the novel is to heighten intensely the overwhelming odds that her heroine, Lutie Johnson must face" (65). Larsen sets up her character Helga in the same manner or perhaps in her own diversion from a circle of "girlfriends" and unconsciously acts this out in characterizing Helga whose history is much like her own. Thadious M. Davis notes that during Larsen's time as a nursing student at New York's Lincoln Hospital, one of her female classmates had observed that Larsen " 'was not at all home with those around her' " (78). In Davis' view, "Larsen's time in the nurses' dormitory was also a missed opportunity for female bonding, for she formed no lasting friendship with any of her nursing peers" (78–79).

By connecting and sharing with other black women, African American women have a chance for survival. For both Helga and Lutie as female protagonists, the necessity to move to the fourth phase of the Transient Woman is clear. Such a move explains why female connection and bonding are essential in fighting against annihilation. As offered earlier, female identity and autonomy are not realized by separating oneself from others. The strength of female relationships is imperative in female selfhood as Lorde asserts that "it is through the coming together of self-actualized individuals…that any real advances can be made" (46). For in the circle of like women, they can share like experiences and nurture one another in self-growth and female resilience. Thus, the fourth phase, Digression, makes it possible for black women to form their own defenses in Third Space before moving back into the dominant culture's space.

Demystifying the American Dream

Helga Crane's and Lutie Johnson's final outcomes show the connection between materiality, places of location, and the disruption of black female consciousness. Centering economics and class, *Quicksand* and *The Street*, through the demise of Helga and Lutie, explore the social evils of classism and materialism that impede African American women's thinking. Larsen opens *Quicksand* with a sense of Helga's misplaced values in focusing on Helga Crane's room filled with costly furnishings of the middle class. Helga's room contains a blue Chinese carpet, "a shining brass bowl" with multicolored nasturtiums, a "stool with oriental silk," and a dark tapestry "high-back chair" (Larsen 2). Helga's exquisite taste is manifested in her expensive clothes: her loungewear consists of "vivid green and gold negligee and glistening brocaded mules" (2). Explicitly, Helga's existence and self-esteem include and depend on possessions that give her a forged sense of security.

Showing Helga's love for fine objects and clothes, the novel suggests Helga's false sense of self and her inability to think clearly. In the opening scene, Helga appears in the above loungewear "want[ing] forgetfulness, complete mental relaxation, rest from thought of any kind" (2). Helga gains comfort and some sense of escape from her common life at Naxos when she is costumed to exhibit wealth and status.

Helga's love of clothes and desire to please others cloud her thinking about the personal change she seeks. When Helga is introduced to Denmark society, she is all too ready to satisfy her aunt's longing for her to dress against her own taste in clothes. Helga allows others to objectify her as something only to be viewed as different. Her aunt tells her,

> "Oh, I'm an old married lady, and a Dane. But you, you're young. And you're a foreigner, and different. You must have bright things to set off the color of your lovely brown skin. Striking things, exotic things. You must make an impression." (68)

Helga's worship of expensive and lovely things is part of the driving force that pushes her outside the realm of critical thinking and disallows her from seeing that her aunt and others view her as something "foreign…and different." When others view her in this way, Helga is made into an object, as entity with no emotions or capacity for thought. No longer is she able to conceive "liberatory paradigms of black subjectivity" as required for complete female development (hooks, *Yearning* 18).

Money, wealth, and ego orchestrate Helga's ruin. Larsen focuses on Helga's fixation with money and its problems when she writes,

> [Helga] hated to admit that money was the most serious difficulty. Knowing full well that it was important, she nevertheless rebelled at the unalterable truth that it could influence her actions, block her desires. A sordid necessity to be grappled with. With Helga, it was almost a superstition that to concede to money its importance magnified its power. (6)

Money is a weakness for Helga. Having focused on the shallow attention she was given by her aunt's social group, Helga gives up her black identity and her sense of worth while taking pleasure in the attention heaped upon her. The narrator explains,

> Incited. That was it, the guiding principle of her life in Copenhagen. She was incited to make an impression. She was incited to inflame attention and admiration. She was dressed for it, subtly schooled for it. And after a little while she gave herself wholly to the fascinating business of being seen, gaped at, desired. Against the solid background of Herr Dahl's wealth and generosity she submitted to her aunt's arrangement of her life to one end, the amusing one of being noticed and flattered. (74)

The attention, admiration, and wealth in Denmark help plunge Helga into her eventual self-ruin. Essentially, materiality gives her a false sense of self.

Unlike Helga, who has money, Lutie Johnson is driven to the end of her existence by her poverty. Because of her family's lack of a means of support and because of her status as an unskilled black woman, Lutie takes a job as a maid to the wealthy Chandler family. Her position as maid and being away from home begin the end of her marriage, family, and self:

> She'd been washing someone else's dishes when she should have been home with Jim and Bub. Instead she'd cleaned another woman's house and looked after another woman's child while her marriage went to pot; [her psyche] breaking up into so many little pieces it couldn't be put back together again, couldn't even be patched into a vague resemblance of its former self. (Petry 30)

If there had been a job for Jim and money to pay their bills, Lutie's chances of survival as a whole person, mother, and wife might have been possible. The problem is not so much that Lutie takes a job away from home, but it is the same circumstance that "drove [her] father to drink and [her] mother to her early grave...that [*sic*] Lutie Johnson was determined that [*sic*] none of these things would happen to her" (107–109). Lutie's determination to have a better life for herself and son outside the one in which the hegemony has placed her is displaced by disrupt cultural values that are "designed to promote and reinforce domination" (*Yearning* 4).

The conditions and the positions from which African Americans live and struggle are the precise ones that Lutie tries not to live. The narrator recounts the hopelessness in Lutie's black community:

> It was a bad street. . . . It was any street where people were packed together like sardines in a can. . . . It was any place where the women had to work to support the families because the men couldn't get jobs and the men got bored and pulled out and the kids were left without proper homes because there was nobody around to put a heart into it. Yes. It was any place where people were so damn poor they didn't have time to do anything but work. . . . [,] where the crowding together made the young girls wise beyond their years. (206)

Without doubt, the conditions in which Lutie exists are distressing. However, Petry's novel points to choices African Americans have in removing themselves from an impoverished existence and physical surroundings that need not define spiritual identity.

Lutie's idea of pursing the American Dream blurs other ways of removing her and Bub from their disadvantaged circumstances. Working and living with the white family, Lutie absorbs their values, believing she can have the same existence they have. The narrator discloses Lutie's thinking:

> After a year of listening to their talk, she absorbed some of the same spirit. The belief that anybody could be rich if he wanted to and worked hard enough and figured it out carefully enough. Apparently that's what the Prizzinis had done. She and Jim could do the same thing, and she thought she saw what had been wrong with them before—they hadn't tried hard enough, worked long enough, saved enough. There hadn't been any one thing they wanted above and beyond everything else. These people had wanted only one thing—more and more money— and so they got it. Some of this new philosophy crept into her letters to Jim. (43)

After her move to Harlem, Lutie soon realizes that the little money she makes or saves will not remove her from the hardships of being black and female. Petry writes,

> She had wanted an apartment to herself and she got it. And now looking down at the accumulation of rubbish, she was suddenly appalled, for she didn't know what the next step would be. She hadn't thought any further than the apartment. Would they have to go on living here year after year? With just enough money to buy food and clothes and to see an occasional movie? What happened next? (74)

The American Dream becomes just what it implies—a dream, a disguised truth. The myth of owning property and having a well-paying job is a paradox for Lutie and other blacks.

Again, according to Lutie's foggy thinking, only by obtaining money and wealth can she escape the status assigned to her by dominant society, of being black, female, and poor. Realizing that she cannot exist on her meager salary, Lutie makes the mistake of slipping into another dream—the entertainment world. Unlike other young black women who "had an urgent hunger for companionship" that the Junto bar offered, "men of all sizes and descriptions," Lutie "was going there so that she could for a moment capture the illusion of having some of the things she lacked" (144). Christian adds about Lutie taking a nightclub job and that "Petry invokes a developing stereotype—that of the black woman singer. But again Lutie finds that talent is not enough and that her only saleable commodity is sex" (*Black Women* 66). However, "Lutie's insistence on her moral standards results in her destruction. She kills Boots, her potential employer, when he tries to rape her" (Christian, *Black Women* 66). Lutie learns late that, similar to how others viewed her as a sexualized object working for the Chandlers, Junto and Boots consider her for work only in the sexual realm. Nonetheless, Petry tries to invoke the idea that Lutie still has other choices for work besides the one that keeps her away from her son at night.

LOCATING SAFE SPACE FOR SURVIVAL AND RENEWAL

As seen in the examples of the characters remaining at the center of dominant discourse, the fourth phase of the Transient

Woman—Flight—is not realized for Helga and Lutie. Here, the importance of Third Space requires movement away from hegemonic oppression. Helga's move from Naxos and Lutie's move from the Chandlers' white space are futile in making any authentic significant changes to their lives. Helga's first stop in her travels is Chicago, where Helga begins her journey toward finding herself. It becomes her "in-between" space before traveling north to Harlem, Denmark, and finally back to the South. In the windy city, Helga faces her black identity when she pays a visit to Uncle Peter's "old stone house." The old stone house as a metaphor implies hegemony's rigidness in defining race and identity. Larsen portrays in the imagery of the maid "dressed primly in black and white" the "mistrust" Helga has in her own mixed ancestry (Larsen 28). The mistrust in her identity is further enhanced when Helga meets Uncle Peter's new wife who unfeelingly expresses that Uncle Peter really is not her uncle as her "mother wasn't married" to her father (29). Helga's ambiguous identity is further exploited by white dominance when she tries to find work but needs "references" (33). Reference, in this sense, implies that Helga as a black woman needs authentication of her existence.[6]

Helga's time in Harlem and Denmark further extends the uncertainty of her racial and female identity. Mrs. Hayes-Rore warns her about being isolated and alienated in New York: " 'New York's the lonesomest place in the world if you don't know anybody' " (40). However, a year past her arrival in Harlem, Helga believes she has found a place where she might have a better future as a black woman:

> In the actuality of the pleasant present and the delightful vision of an agreeable future she was contented, and happy. She did not analyze this contentment, this happiness, but vaguely, without putting it into words or even so tangible a thing as a thought, she knew it sprang from a sense of freedom, a release from the feeling of smallness which had hedged her in, first during her sorry, unchildlike childhood among hostile white folk in Chicago, and later during her uncomfortable sojourn among snobbish black folk in Naxos. (46)

In hegemonic space, Helga believes she can finally find happiness. Nevertheless, without sufficient self-knowledge, Helga is doomed to repeat the mistakes in finding a location where she might realize her fullest potential as a black woman. Larson shows this false sense in Helga before she moves to Denmark and is overtaken by a fear of blacks. Unconsciously, Helga wishes to remove herself from persons or places that remind her of her black identity. Lost in her thinking of who she is as another African American, Helga considers,

> Abruptly it flashed upon her that the harrowing irritation of the past weeks was a smoldering hatred. Then, she was overcome by another, so actual, so sharp, so horribly painful, that forever afterwards she preferred to forget it. It was as if she were shut up, boxed up, with hundreds of her race, closed up with the something in the racial character which had always been, to her, inexplicable, alien. Why, she demanded in fierce rebellion, should she be yoked to these despised black folk? (54–55)

In Helga's blurred vision, she returns to her earlier thinking that prompted her to leave Naxos. Helga mixes the idea of conformity with her idea of one's location within race. It is conformity she wishes to move away from, but she negates the value of being in specific places with one's racial family.

Helga moves to Denmark "to free herself from fear of suffocation" with blacks (Christian, *Black Women* 52). However, her departure to Denmark places her in the racial "box" from which she runs away in America. As an Other in Denmark, Helga is a "curiosity, a stunt," "a decoration. A curio. A peacock," and "some disgusting sensual creature" (Larsen 71, 73, 89). Helga has no real sense of self and no good judgment of what she wants.

Likewise, Lutie Johnson's failure to depart from 116th Street to Third Space prevents possible alliances with like African American women. Despite Lutie's good intentions to fight the societal odds against her and Bub, Petry shows the limitations placed on black women outside a space of female support. Petry sets up this idea with the humanlike qualities of the wind in the "street." As Christian notes, "The heroine of this period, Lutie Johnson...[is] defeated both by social reality and by [her] lack of knowledge. Self-knowledge was critical if black women were to develop the inner sources they would need in order to cope with large social forces" (Christian, "Trajectories" 237). Hence, self-knowledge is learned from other females who have experienced like situations in oppression and domination.

In this novel, oppression acquires the form of the wind, which takes on physical and psychological qualities of oppressive hierarchies that limit black women like Lutie in white society. The wind is the larger "invisible and naturalist force[s] behind the street" (Pryse, "Pattern" 122) that embodies the attitudes and indifferences of hegemony. Petry describes the effects of 116th Street, as Lutie's adversary, and the bleak future it holds for Lutie in this space:

> There was a cold November wind blowing through 116th Street. It *rattled* tops of garbage cans, *sucked* window shades out through the top of opened windows and set flapping back against the windows; and it drove most of the people off the street in the block between Seventh and Eighth Avenues except for a few hurried pedestrians who bent double in an effort to offer the least possible exposed surface to its violent assault. (*emphasis added*) (1–2)

The wind "hem[s] Lutie and the others, particularly the women, into that 'ever-narrowing space'" (123), which makes it difficult for them to exist:

> It did everything it could to discourage the people walking along the street. It found all the dirt and dust and grime on the sidewalk and lifted it up so that the dirt got into their noses, making it difficult to breathe; the dust got into their eyes and blinded them.... It wrapped newspaper around their feet entangling them until the people cursed deep in their throats.... The wind blew it back again and again until they were forced to stoop and dislodge the paper with their hands. (Petry 2)

In its attack, the wind uses language, as in the image of newspaper, to confuse blacks. The definition of "created equal" as written by the Founding Fathers in the Declaration of Independence did not include blacks. The wind, in the imagery of the Declaration of Independence, "force[s]" blacks to "stoop" to a lower position. In its violent state, the wind exposes Lutie.

It even makes her vulnerable to its power. As a foreshadowing of Super Jones's sexual assault on Lutie, the wind attacks Lutie:

> The wind lifted Lutie Johnson's hair away from the back of her neck so that she felt suddenly naked and bald....She shivered as the cold fingers of the wind touched the back of her neck, explored the sides of her head. It even blew her eyelashes away from her eyes so that her eyeballs were bathed in a rush of coldness and she had to blink in order to read the words on the sign swaying back and forth over her head.
>
> Each time she thought she had the sign in focus, the wind pushed it away from her so that she wasn't certain whether it said three rooms or two rooms. (2)

The wind in all its power, like hegemony, destroys African Americans. From the description Petry draws in the opening, one senses that it is almost impossible to escape the despair, violence, and brutality that "the street" hegemony inflicts on African Americans.

The spaces and locations that Helga and Lutie inhabit are not productive and meaningful. Each move they make only leads to another disaster. Black women existing in spaces or locations that keep them on the margins are destroyed, unless they locate sites wherein they can thrive as whole subjects. Larsen and Petry present stories that recognize the repression of black women's lives. Their novels show the social conflicts that Helga and Lutie face as African American women and the self-imposed impossibilities of their escape. Larsen concentrates on the tension of identity and female sexuality for Helga in places that perpetuate stereotypes of black women. Helga seeks her identity as a passionate black woman, but the result of each move ends in disappointment. Petry's novel is tragic, with a black woman murdering a black man in self-defense and with an African American woman's defeat in hegemonic oppression. As Christian notes, "Petry is more concerned with proving...no matter how American a poor black person may be, she will be defeated by her environment" (*Black Women* 67). Lutie's problem is that she makes the wrong choices and pursues the wrong models through the illusory American Dream. In this context, places of location that perpetuate hegemony's practices make black female survival and wholeness impossible. As hooks asserts,

> Assimilation, imitation, or assuming the role of rebellious exotic other are not the only available options and never have been. This is why it is crucial to radically revise notions of identity politics, to explore marginal locations as spaces where we can best become whatever we want to be while remaining committed to liberatory black liberation struggle. (*Yearning* 20)

Marginal, in this context, is synonymous with Third Space. If there are chances for black women's survival and wholeness as well as possibilities of envisioning female subjectivity, a move from hegemonic sites is necessary.

5

PRAISESONG FOR THE WIDOW: CROSSING LOCATION AND SPACE TOWARD FEMALE CONSCIOUSNESS AND WHOLENESS

She began to make plans and to dream delightful dreams of change, of life somewhere else. Some place where at last she would be permanently satisfied. Her anticipatory thoughts waltzed and eddied about to the sweet silent music of change. With rapture almost, *she let herself drop into the blissful sensation of visualizing herself in different, strange places, among approving and admiring people, where she would be appreciated, and understood.*

—Nella Larsen[1]

The warmth, the stinging sensation that was both pleasure and pain passed up through the emptiness at her center. Until finally they reached her heart. And as they encircled her heart and it responded, there was the sense of a chord being struck. All the tendons, nerves and muscles which strung her together had been struck a powerful chord, and the reverberation could be heard in the remotest corners of her body.

—Paule Marshall[2]

Larsen's quoted passage above in many ways articulates and suggests a main idea of the Transient Woman model: finding locations where black women can realize female wholeness. Having been silenced and made invisible on the border of hegemonic society, black women, as does Helga Crane in *Quicksand*, find strength in looking toward a "change" in their role and status in dominant society. Along with freedom to express and "visualize" themselves in safe communities "where [they] could be appreciated, and understood" (57), finding spaces for culmination where transformation is possible is a continuing theme, dream, and aspiration of African American women and black women writers alike.

Marshall's *Praisesong for the Widow* (1983) features a black woman, Avatara "Avey" Johnson, who is moving to familiar places to reclaim and reconnect with her ancestral past. Most significantly, Avey's literal and metaphorical movements show the process toward healing her damaged psyche after the trappings of materiality.

As in *Quicksand* and *The Street, Praisesong for the Widow* concerns with the trappings of "materialism, assimilationism, and their erosion of connections with the community, the past, one's self" and with the requirement of personal healing for female consciousness and wholeness (DeLamotte, *Places* 81). Implicitly, the themes of materialism, assimilationism, and identity are connected with places of location and spaces for female realization. Because Marshall's early beginnings were outside the United States and because her family had to make significant changes to their way of living in order to adjust to the American way of life, Marshall draws attention to the deterioration of familial values, ancestral history, and personal identity when black women become fixed on materiality and acculturation. The issues Marshall examines in the text are the ones she and her family faced and considered in their transition to the States.

The connection of familial history and female identity, in fact, is a focus for Marshall, as underscored in the Amiri Baraka quote she uses to begin her story:

> I wanted to know my mother when she sat looking sad across the campus in the late 1920s into the future of the soul, there were black angels straining above her head, carrying life from the ancestors, and knowledge, and the strong nigger feeling.... (epigraph as quoted in *Praisesong* 8)

Like Baraka, Marshall understands the anxieties and problems her mother and the women before her faced as black women in a foreign country that despised and negated the legitimacy of their very presence. Without the help and direction of "black angels" or without black women bringing to the core of their souls or spirits the history, the awareness, and essence of their ancestors, she and others might not have survived such a hostile environment. In Avey's story, the dismissal of her old aunt's wisdom, her fixation on middle-class values, specifically materialism, lead Avey to move from white-centered space to locations that open her connections to her ancestral history and female erotic as described by Lorde. Fundamentally, Marshall's *Praisesong for the Widow* reflects the interconnection of materiality with the break or rupture of Avey Johnson's personal history and female identity.

IDENTITY, MATERIALITY, AND MARRIAGE

"Black women attaining power, authority, and material goods through marriage" (Pettis 24) is a common theme for black women writers. While the marriage plot has been coded as "white, female, and European," African American women writers, as duCille asserts, appropriated the literary form "for their own emancipatory purposes...as a trope to explore [also] complex questions of sexuality and female subjectivity" (3–4). As I explore the critical questions on black women's identity through the critical lens of black female subjectivity, I look at the places and the means by which black women attempt to redefine themselves and realize autonomy in marriage by answering the following questions: Can female consciousness and transformation be realized alongside marriage and materiality? How do upward mobility and materialism create tension for a black female in relation to black female consciousness? To examine Marshall's text on female identity and female wholeness, this chapter also looks at questions regarding personal history in connection with the effects of materiality, including the following: What community or space must African American women inhabit for complete female transformation? How does personal history, specifically one's ancestral history, help in the move back into hegemonic space after female transformation? If early African American women writers used the theme of marriage and materialism as a means for black women to achieve power, authority, and subjectivity, then these questions need to be answered if we are to understand the formation of new identities and female agency for African American women.

TREATMENT OF MARRIAGE AND IDENTITY IN EARLY AFRICAN AMERICAN WOMEN WRITINGS

Hopkins's focus on African Americans seeking acculturation and white values in *Contending Forces* is a major issue for some in understanding why Hopkins includes these in her text. Robert Bone contends that Hopkins subscribes to the myth of white superiority (14). Houston Baker argues that her use of light-skinned characters reflects "an implicit approval of white patriarchy" (25). Likewise, Christian agrees with the others that Hopkins writes "under the influence of whiteness" (as quoted in duCille 7). While it is true that Hopkins incorporates middle-class values in her novel, her basic focus is racial and gender uplift. Her intent is made evident in her preface, to do all she can "in a humble way to raise the stigma of degradation from her race" (Hopkins 13). Implicitly, Hopkins's attention to bourgeois practices, professional occupations, and the middle class is masking her desire to raise the status of black women. Besides employing education in the text as a key for blacks to attain racial equality, Hopkins also understands that marriage, as a sign of civility, can be instrumental for black women's "uplift." duCille convincingly asserts that nineteenth-century black women writers "were propelled not by an accommodationist desire to assimilating and promoting the values of the dominant culture," as suggested by critics' censure, "but by a profoundly political urge to rewrite those patriarchal strictures" (32). Understandably, it is not surprising that Hopkins would connect marriage in her novel to improving black women's chances in society. Hopkins's novel, then, is not intended to promote bourgeois practices but to add to nineteenth-century dialogue about racial justice and sexual equality, specifically, black female autonomy.

How may marriage and acquiring middle-class values realize black female identity and subjectivity? In the matter of femininity, black women used marriage as entry into dominant society. As advocates of "racial uplift" in their works and their way of living, black women at the turn of century wanted to be on equal footing with their white female counterparts by way of cultural refinement, beauty, and marriage. While some may argue that physical beauty and matrimony were not the only means to attain "equal footing," it was practical for black women writers to use these in changing images of black women as unrefined and unvirtuous following slavery.

Using marriage as an underlying theme in *Contending Forces*, Hopkins shows through John and Grace Montfort's union that marriage offers protection for women. When John Pollock openly expresses his feelings as more than friendship to Grace, she quickly reminds him that his friendship is with her husband and that if he continues making advances at her she will report his actions to her husband. As a married woman, Grace understands that the protection her husband provides removes her from the gaze of other males. Besides offering economic security to a woman, marriage also provides, as in this scenario, a safeguard in protecting woman's virtues as honorable woman and wife.

Marriage in *Contending Forces* secures for a black woman a respectable reputation and position in black Boston society. Dora is engaged to the prominent attorney John Langley. Though not liked by some in the community, Langley is respected as an attorney for his skills and for having a promising future in politics. Because he is competent in law and debate, Langley can potentially campaign for social equality and justice for the black Bostonians. With Langley in marriage, opportunities will likely open for Dora to further develop herself while working beside him for civil justice.

An outstanding feature about marriage in Hopkins's novel, unlike those in usual sentimental novels, is that marriage offers agency for the female heroine. In the case of Dora and Sappho, marriage allows for female autonomy. After returning from England, Dora and Sappho secure teaching positions, alongside their spouses, as a means to lifting their race in the South (401). Different from white heroines in marriage who are placed in the domestic realm or space, Dora and Sappho gain independence by continuing to work in the public sphere. Marriage as expressed by nineteenth-century black women writers situates marriage as a sign of progress and "is the site for women to carry out the convictions of exemplary black citizenship" (Tate, *Domestic Allegories* 125). Such actions and activities affirm Hopkins' heroines' desire to be active players in lifting the race as well as to exhibit characteristics of committed and passionate women.

Black female desire for materiality, in Hopkins's novel, is a sign of female propriety and developed appreciation for the aesthetics of the home. The Smith family is cultured and reflects appreciation of fine furnishings for their home. Hopkins, in fact, spends much time in describing Ma Smith's childhood home:

> [The] floors were covered with carpet as no housekeeper was counted much who did not have a large supply of such things. There were china figures on the mantel, and vases filled with golden-rod.... The furniture was mahogany, polished until you could see your face in any part of it. There was a red cloth on the table...and in the center of it was a large astral lamp trimmed about the edges with long crystal penchants, which [the] children called diamonds. (93)

Ma Smith's present home is furnished similarly. The homes Hopkins describes here are ones filled with beautiful and valued things. Such furnishings point to a black middle-class family unlike the past deprived black class who often lived in homes barely furnished. Hopkins makes no excuse for those African Americans who desire the same as whites in wanting to "give their children...a few of the refinements of living" (86). She says that "whatever grace or accomplishment may be the order of the hour, it is copied or practiced among some portion of the colored population" (Hopkins 86). Granted the homes Hopkins describes in her text are not inhabited by the masses; however, they do mark a radical change from white nineteenth-century depictions of how blacks existed. Moreover, the Victorian-type furnished homes in the novel show, as Hopkins comments, "the steady advance of a race overriding the barriers set by prejudice and injustice" (87).

Like Hopkins, Larsen explores the issue of material acquisition and marriage in *Quicksand* and *Passing*. However, the question of marriage and materiality includes beauty, for exercising black female agency is viewed differently in the latter. Here

Larsen extends the discussion and looks at the effects of materialism and marriage on the psyche of black women, especially fair-skinned females. Larsen's heroines, like Hopkins', have long hair, thin facial features, style, and poise. They resemble white females and pass as such. As married black women passing in white circles, Christian suggests, they gain freedom in movement to cross racial and class lines. On biracial women marrying for status, Christian comments,

> The passer is often a woman who believes that through her marriage to a wealthy white man, she might gain economic security and more freedom of mobility. The process of passing could have peculiarly feminine overtones, for a woman can often cement her future according to the man she marries. (*Black Women* 45)

The problem in Christian's analysis is the danger in the discovery of the woman's true identity and the potential loss of her economic security in marriage. Moreover, in this case, the woman's movement is excluded from the circles where she once enjoyed membership and privilege.

The issues of black female identity and economic security in marriage are particularly revealing in *Passing*. Though the issue of being discovered in passing is not the problem for Helga Crane in *Quicksand,* she does portray the black female protagonist Christian speaks about in being absorbed with materialism. Larsen, in fact, spends a fair amount of time in the beginning of the novel setting up Helga as a person who loves beautiful and rare things. In Demark where she lives among the upper class, Helga has everything "she had wanted … [,] the things which money could give, leisure, attention, beautiful surroundings. Things. Things. Things" (Larsen 67). Materiality, in this sense and in Denmark, subjects Helga to functioning as "a peacock. A curio" (73). Larsen reveals that despite Helga's freedom of movement because of the money she has in Denmark, she is ensnared by a false sense of identity and independence.

Black female identity, marriage, and class are also contested in *Passing*. In the novel, Irene Redfield and Clare Kendry acquire material goods and freedom of social movement when they marry men of position. Through "passing," Clare Kendry marries a white wealthy man for identity and class. Irene Redfield marries an African American physician for status and movement in the black social circles of Harlem. Both women, through marriage and material acquisition, seek to raise their status from socially unaccepted black women to visibly white women with power in status and wealth. Despite their short-lived success as elitist women, Larsen demonstrates, as Christian notes, that light-skinned heroines are not class or race free even "in conventional, urban, upper-class... [and] rural" societies (*Black Women* 53).

Like Larsen, Hurston criticizes class-seeking and its effects in her account of Janie's years of marriage in *Their Eyes Were Watching God*. In her second marriage, Janie weds a man who accumulates wealth and property after he is made mayor of the all-black town in Florida. Like the previous mulattoes, Janie is viewed by men as just that—a light-skinned, long-haired exotic female. As Christian points out, Jody "forcibly installs her as Queen of the Porch and cuts her off from any real contact with their community. She becomes his showpiece, his property" (*Black Women* 59). As women attain class and material goods through marriage, they paradoxically become objects in exchange for security.

Unlike Helga and Irene, Janie does not marry for status or freedom of mobility. She marries Jody because she is repulsed by her first husband, Logan Killicks, whom she is forced to marry by her grandmother for social and financial security. Janie thinks Jody might "represent sun-up and pollen and blooming trees," and that she might find marriage as "the sanctum of a bloom" and the "ecstatic shiver of the tree from root to tiniest branch creaming in every blossom and frothing with delight" (Hurston 10–11). However marriage, status as "Queen," and owning things remove Janie from a natural context and do not satisfy her. As Pettis points out, Janie "benefits from sharing in [Jody's] accomplishments, however, [they] stymie her development and cause psychic division" (24). Critically, Hurston and Larsen look at and show the artificiality of queen-like positions and "question the value of satisfying a woman's ambitions through means that are not self-generated" (Pettis 24).

Do these marriages allow for personal development and subjectivity?[3] Some argue that Hopkins writes her novel in the tradition of the sentimental novel with a marriage at the end. Although this might be the case, the major difference between white marriages in sentimental fiction, however, is that Hopkins's version of marriage in *Contending Forces* allows her female character to exercise autonomy; she moves freely with her husband across space (America to England and then back to the South) to work jointly in educating their people. She is not confined to the assigned woman's spaces of the house, the kitchen, for example. In Clare's and Irene's marriages, there are possibilities of movement into wider social circles in and outside Harlem, however, personal issues of jealousy and resentment toward the other's marriage prevent each from developing in moral fiber and as women. On the other hand, Hurston's Janie, by virtue of her demonstrated resistance and independence, shows female subjectivity. According to Pettis, "Janie achieves unquestionable autonomy, for example, only when she is manless, thus confirming that whatever power and authority she owns are independent of male origination or support" (25). Indeed, Janie demonstrates autonomous power without marriage and materiality and acquires her own "voice," through her narrative relationship with Phoeby, to articulate and name her own experiences.

Trappings of Class Consciousness

Like the previous works, Marshall's *Praisesong for the Widow* demonstrates how upward mobility and materiality create tension in the female psyche. Besides Hurston's *Their Eyes Were Watching God* and "The Gilded Six-Bits," Marshall's *Praisesong for the Widow* is perhaps one of the few works by black women writers that examines the effects of materialism on the psyche and physical body of African American women and resolves those effects in a positive way. Although works by African American women before Marshall look at the intersection of race, class, and gender in relation to black women, Marshall writes and comments on women who have fallen into the trap of materialism and who now need a physical and psychological cleansing to rejuvenate their female psyche. Avey Johnson, a middle-aged widow, is such a woman who must be absolved of her obsessive American materialism and returned to her ancestral roots and values if she is to define herself as a black woman. Particularly interesting is Marshall's use of African elements in relation to black women's sense of self. Like the women in Walker's *The Color Purple*, Marshall's women use physical movement from one place to another to enhance and put into perspective their true visions of themselves as black women. In *The Color Purple*, Nettie moves from the U.S. South to Africa and back again; in *Praisesong*, Avey moves from White Plains in New York to Carriacou and back to the United States. Through Avey, Marshall shows that the removal of the psychological restraints on the black female spirit must materialize in places outside the borders of America. Movement to places of location is important for this discussion, and so is a consideration of mobility from one class to another and its effects.

Praisesong for the Widow is a black female's narrative about spiritual reawakening and regeneration. In the novel, Avatara "Avey" Johnson has lost connection with her ancestral roots and with herself as a black woman. Avey has unconsciously absorbed the spirit of Western culture and fallen into the trap of class consciousness, which includes focusing on materialistic values and ideas. For Avey, materialism becomes a spiritual and psychological problem, since this focus completely supplants her black roots. For Avey to return to herself as a black woman, she must undergo a renewal or restoration to heal her fragmented psyche. The process of healing consists of calling up memories of past relationships with female ancestors and includes a physical and psychological cleansing of the individual spirit and mind. Christian explains, "Marshall emphasizes the seemingly irrational ways in which the collective memory of black people has a hold on the Avey Johnsons of America" ("Trajectories" 245). While African Americans may progress in class status, the remembrance of where they come from and how they have arrived at this new place in modern society remains with the black spirit even when it has long been buried under middle-class values and personal corruption. Eugenia DeLamotte writes that

the materialism that imprisons Avey in silence and stasis by the time of her third Caribbean cruise on the *Bianca Pride* is not a sin but a form of violence a racist economy has inflicted on her, first through poverty and then through the fierce struggle against it that deadened her husband with self-alienating work. (82)

The silence and stasis to which DeLamotte refers are the result of the power of the American economic system to exploit and oppress the marginalized, particularly African Americans. For Avey, the silence and stasis drain her female spirit and erotic. When the erotic, which resides in a "spiritual female plane," is consumed by materialism, the female is disjoined from the power source that prevents her annihilation. As Lorde contends,

> There are many kinds of power, used and unused, acknowledged or otherwise. The erotic is a resource within each of us that lies in a deeply female and *spiritual plane*, firmly rooted in the power of our unexpressed or unrecognized feeling. In order to perpetuate itself, every oppression must corrupt or distort those various sources of power within the culture of the oppressed that can provide energy for change. For women, this has meant a suppression of the erotic as a considered source of power and information within our lives. (*emphasis added*) (53)

Indeed, materiality and its effects are the oppressive forces that "corrupt" and leave Avey empty of feeling her true self and disconnected from her roots as a black woman, particularly in a society that views and treats her as an object. The power of materialism, as Lorde sees it, can develop and exist only if women like Avey provide its power through material and cultural consumption.

The novel also explores Avey's and Jay's relationship and the effects of material consumption on their marriage. The beginning of Avey and Jay's marriage, though they are financially impoverished, consists of mutual love and understanding. Without the need for money for good times together, as in the past, Avey and Jay share the better times in their marriage with natural ease. In these times, their love flows.

However, the strain of bringing up children, living in close quarters, and Jay's simultaneous jobs take a toll on the marriage. Jay is absorbed with finding ways to make money; he begins "reading books on career building, personality improvement, selling techniques, business English and the like" (113). The excessive time spent away from Avey does not help much in keeping the marriage fulfilled.

Jay's obsession with work and the American Dream puts a strain on the marriage when Avey suspects Jay is unfaithful. Jay works in a department store, which puts him in a position of relating closely with white female coworkers. Repelled by living in Brooklyn, Avey redirects her hurt and begins a quest for the American Dream, pressuring Jay to provide a house. In this sense, Avey disconnects her feelings from the actual problem and places it in the realm of owning things. Taken with the problems in her marriage, Avey is separated from her sense of self and fails to depend on her erotic power to realize that her dilemma is connected to race, gender, and class. If Avey understands how hegemonic oppression works, she might understand that the American Dream is not available in the same way to African Americans.

Marshall focuses on the threat of materiality and its effect on Avey and Jay Johnson as a black couple. Jay's fixation on working several jobs and getting a college degree gets to the point where he "put on blinders to shut out anything...that might prove distracting, and thus cause him...to break his stride" (115). In Jay's mind, the only important thing is working and getting money to buy the things that say he is a self-made man. Even the things that had been essential to him to share with Avey no longer take precedence. The record-playing, dancing, and the ritual of playfulness "found themselves on the sidelines, out of his line of vision" (115).

Like Jay, Avey turns away from her marriage and is not concerned with the changes in her marriage or those she finds in herself. As Marshall points out,

> Avey scarcely noticed the changes, she was kept so much on the run. Or more truthfully, she noticed them but did not dare to stop and reflect; there was no time for that kind of thing, she told herself; there was just too much else she had to do. (116)

If she stops to consider their deteriorating marriage, Avey would have to face the truth that part of the fault lies with her wanting to buy things. Marshall shows that Avey uses her job away from home to escape from her own marital problems: She is glad that what she does is just a job, something that pays her a salary while leaving her to her own thoughts most of the day. Anything else would have been too much (117). Avey is in denial about her failing marriage and uses her job away from her home and children as an escape. She uses her idle time to plan for the suburban home that she thinks will remove the problems with Jay:

> *Her mind shifting, she began dreaming* as usual of the day when they would be able to move from Halsey Street into a larger apartment on another block, a clean, quiet, tree-lined block with no trolley.…they might be able to rent the basement and parlor floor of a brownstone. Now that she was working again that might be possible in a few years.…
>
> The thought of the rooms, large, warm, sunny rooms, sustained her through…the hardships. (*emphasis added*) (119)

Even as Avey is thinking of owning a brownstone and more space for her and the children, she is preoccupied with thoughts of how she might obtain extra money by renting out a room of the house. The thoughts she gives to owning property and making money are more a part of her thinking than her understanding of how to fix her marital problems. Avey is disconnected from her self and her marriage.

In representing the struggle for economic security in racist America, Marshall raises questions that point to the thesis of her novel: Can African Americans have both the American Dream and their sense of self? Is it possible for blacks to remain true to their ancestral/African roots while blending with an "American" way of life? Years later after Jay's death does Avey understand how materiality had taken the happiness and security out of their marriage: "All this had passed from their lives without their hardly noticing. There had been not time" (138). She thinks about their consumption of materiality; during a cruise, Avey finally comes to the realization that the Dream had robbed them of their sense of self:

> *Too much!* They had behaved, she and Jay, as if there had been nothing about themselves worth honoring!
>
> *Too much!* Couldn't they have done differently? Hadn't there perhaps been another way? Questions which scarcely had any

shape to them flooded her mind, and she struggled to give them form. Would it have been possible to have done both? (139)

Avey is finally contemplating these questions that mean it is not too late for her, at least to change and reconnect with her self. Marshall answers Avey's questions in the last sections of her novel, providing a look at ancestral history and self-connection.

Ancestral History and Black Female Wholeness

In the second half of the novel, Marshall shows the importance of ancestral history and its relation to black female wholeness in remaining connected to the erotic. Looking at Jay and Avey, Marshall points to the disruption of the self when they are captivated by the appeal of materiality and white middle-class values that are in direct opposition to African roots and values. In the story, Marshall purposely uses symbols of hegemony that disrupt the value system of blackness. In essence, she shows the clash of two opposing value systems that prevents blacks from remaining whole and true to themselves. Living on Halsey Street, for example, Jay and Avey are connected with who they are as blacks. When they lived on Halsey Street as commoners, they "would look forward to the trip to Tatem each summer" for the "down-home life" (116). However, after moving to North White Plains, the desire to remain grounded in their roots is replaced by a taste for comfortable living in white suburban America.

In another instance, the middle-class symbol of cruises propels the destruction of black female characters already disconnected from their roots. For example, while on one of the cruises Avey takes with her friends Thomasina and Clarice, Avey is disgusted with Clarice when during a carnival parade she goes into a dance frenzy with the commoners. Avey is embarrassed at Clarice's "swishing her bony hips to the drums" and resembling "an organ grinder's monkey begging pennies from her shoulders" (25). Avey is humiliated by the perspiring Clarice, especially since "white passengers [were] watching. White faces laughing! White hands applauding! Avey Johnson had never been so mortified" (25). Avey forgets that music and dancing is part of her and her black identity and thinks Clarice is acting only primitively when Clarice responds, " 'Girl, those drums *got* to me!' " (26). In some sense, Avey has appropriated whiteness and judges Clarice as Other.

Marshall investigates the question of history and family and its connection to the inner black female psyche. As someone whose history includes roots in Barbados and the United States, Marshall tries to retrieve the culture that shaped her and the generation of women before her. In writing her novel, Marshall places and moves Avey between two cultures and two locations. Marshall places Avey's history early in the context of old Aunt Cuney whose roots connect with the Ibos who came to the United States as slaves through South Carolina. In this way, Marshall shows that Avey's most fundamental beginnings are primarily her African roots and not her life bounded by white America. Susan Willis, pointing out about black women and their cultural past, notes that "if there is one thing that predominates in contemporary writing by black American women, it is the journey (both real and figural) back to the historical source of the black American community" (58). Marshall uses something of the same form in her novel with Avey. Avey's history begins with her African connections with Aunt Cuney and in this context she must return to this beginning to reclaim that part of her identity she lost in the process of acculturation in white-centered values.

Aunt Cuney and Lebert Joseph are Marshall's most involved ancestral characters in the story who appear as "mythical, timeless, and futuristic visionaries" (Pettis 118). Through Aunt Cuney in her memories, dreams, and visions, and with Lebert Joseph's intervention, Avey reconnects with her past. As Pettis points out about their roles in redirecting Avey, "Aunt Cuney, though literally dead, forces Avey to confront her ravaged spirit. Joseph directs Avey to the island of Carriacou, and through his intercession, Avey reconnects herself culturally" (118). An interesting aspect is the duality of the roles of Aunt Cuney and Lebert with Avey: male/female, present/past, and alive/dead. Aunt Cuney's and Lebert's functions are complementary and, as such, help Avey regain her wholeness.

Aunt Cuney passes to Avey the lessons required of her to remain secure in African roots to protect her from values centered in white society. On her summer visits to the south, Aunt Cuney teaches young Avey the lessons about resistance she learned from their ancestors. The lessons Aunt Cuney teaches are purposeful in teaching Avey how to live in a white world without being consumed by it. Aunt Cuney tells the legendary story of the Ibos and their refusal to assimilate to the local culture in America after they arrive from Africa:

> "The minute those Ibos was brought on shore they just stopped...and take a look around. A good long look. Not saying a word. Just studying the place real good....And they seen things that day you and me don't have the power to see.... [T]hey seen everything that was to happen 'round here that day. The slavery time and the war my gran' always talked about, the 'mancipation and everything....And when they got through sizing up the place...they just turned...all of 'em...and walked on back down to the edge of the river here." (Marshall 37–39)

Aunt Cuney's message is about having control over one's mind when one is powerless to change his or her situation or location. When the Ibos foresaw their condition in America, in their mind, " 'They just kept walking right on out over the river....But chains didn't stop those Ibos none' " (39). Aunt Cuney wants Avey to learn, like the Ibos, how to separate her mental state from her physical body when faced with suppression. Aunt Cuney would tell Avey that even when " 'her body...might be in Tatem...her mind...was long gone with the Ibos' " (39). Though her body is restricted to the oppression around her, Aunt Cuney says her mind, "regardless of her physical location," is free and boundless. The other part of Aunt Cuney's moral lesson is for Avey to take the story with her in life and retell it to the next generation. It is not long after marriage, the ending of family trips to Tatem, and the accumulating of possessions that Avey forgets to pass the story on to her children. Moreover, Avey fails to remember Aunt Cuney's lesson in safeguarding her mind when she herself begins deteriorating later in life.

Lebert Joseph functions then as intercessory in bringing Avey back to her African connection. Avey's first impression of

Joseph Lebert is that "he was one of the those old people who give the impression of having undergone a lifetime trial by fire which they somehow managed to turn to their own good in the end; using the fire to burn away everything in them that could possibly decay, everything mortal" (161). Like Aunt Cuney, Lebert is part of the process of learning from which Avey can connect to her past. He has seen life through the eyes of a black man and has learned to make the most of his situation by not falling into the trap of destruction.

Marshall presents Lebert as someone "who possessed ways of seeing that went beyond mere sight and ways of knowing that outstripped ordinary intelligence" (172). Lebert Joseph is Avey's teacher and guide. Lebert "saw how far she had come since leaving the ship and the distance she had yet to go" (172). As DeLamotte points out, Joseph is "a magical, protean figure," a Legba trickster figure who "stands at the crossroads on Carriacou as he waits to escort Avey up the hill to the ceremony; both literally and figuratively he occupies a position at the crossroads of Africa and America" (101). In the role DeLamotte references, Lebert has many connections: Africa and America, the living and the dead worlds, the present and the past, the present and the future generations to come. Lebert is linked to an Africa of both the past and the present and to Avey's present.

Lebert also teaches Avey what family history means, particularly self-identity, and how it sustains him in life: "He was telling her his family history, going on like some Old Testament prophet chronicling the lineage of his tribe" (163). Because Lebert is intuitive in picking up energies from others and senses Avey's fractured state, he asks Avey, "'And what you is?'" "'What's your nation?'" (166, 167). Such questions foreground the issue of subjectivity and suggest that "there is a something" Avey "possesses, has, evokes...that also must be claimed" (Quashie 15). Essentially, it begs from Avey "what or who is this 'you'? 'What are the names and properties' of this you?" (15). Through Lebert's function and connections, Marshall discloses the interconnection of blacks' history with Africa and America and that both are significant in African Americans' identity.[4]

Avey's later reply to Lebert's question about her identity reveals a person who is disconnected from her personal history: " 'I don't know what you are asking me.... I'm a visitor, a tourist, just someone here for the day' " (167). In her disassociation from her past and from the lessons Aunt Cuney gave, Avey is a "tourist"—a foreigner—in her own ancestral land. One of the elements that set Marshall's writing apart from other black women writers' work is her insight concerning the cost to blacks of their cultural disconnection (Pettis 10). With the character of Avey, Marshall shows what happens to black women who are disconnected from themselves because of their privileging of Eurocentric ideas. Marshall's work in *Praisesong* essentially demonstrates the causes and effects of black identity disconnection that results in a fractured psyche.[5]

Hegemonic Influences on the Female Psyche

Marshall provides evidence of the fracturing of Avey's psyche, which is the cause of her breakdown on her excursion. As Pettis points out about fractured psyche, "Fragmentation is located in the historical experiences of black people of the African diaspora, and the fractured psyche is defined as the rending and mutilation of human spirit, a process that represents an unavoidable consequence of traumatic cultural displacement" (3). Such fragmentation is found in Avey, who shows a need for healing and a reconnection with her self as a black woman of African descent. Avey is out of touch with her black reality and her connection with blacks like her. When standing among black passersby in Grenada looking for a cab, Avey is clueless as to why the villagers act as if they know her:

> From the way they [were] acting she could have been simply one of them.... There was a familiarity, almost an intimacy, to their gestures of greeting.... The problem was, she decided, none of them seemed aware of the fact that she was a stranger, a visitor, a tourist, although this should have been obvious from the way she was dressed and the set of matching luggage at her side. (Marshall 69)

Avey visualizes herself as a foreigner and not as one of them. She is, in fact, a "foreigner" estranged from her own understanding of herself as a black woman.

It is not merely Avey who sees herself as different and disassociated from the black villagers, some of the people around her too see her as Other. Avey has lost her "self-regard" in the sense of her inability to see herself "from a vantage point outside the self" (DeLamotte, *Places* 91). Her perspective is limited, just as that of the taxi driver in Grenada; he understands Avey from the way she presents herself—"Looking up into the mirror he appeared to take a quick inventory of her" (75)—and appraises her from the clothes she wears as if she is an "object" in a store window for public gaze, as Avey has often viewed herself.

Aunt Cuney's dream might have been a wake-up call for Avey to reflect on her African American heritage. During the cruise with a largely white population on board the *Bianca Pride* (which translates to white pride), Avey cannot recognize the mirror reflection of herself as a black woman. Looking at a likeness in the dining room mirror, "She easily recognized [her companions] in the distant mirror. But for a long confused moment Avey Johnson could not place the woman [herself] in beige crepe de Chine and pearls seated with them" (48). Acting and dressing as white middle-class, Avey again does not recognize herself. When Avey mentions to her doctor what some might call as an out-of-body experience, he laughs and says "a sure sign…of money in the bank" (49). Marshall's concern with the effects of materialism attests to her recognition of the outcome for other blacks like Avey.

On other occasions, Avey's fragmented state propels her to believe she is seeing someone outside herself and that it is another person. One time when shopping and looking in the store's floor mirror, Avey believes she sees another woman's reflection when in fact it is her own. Avey "notice[s] a black woman of above average height with a full-figured yet compact body coming toward her amid the floor-length mirrors down the aisle. And in the way she always did she would quickly note the stranger's clothes" (48). The stranger seems to follow her; she sees the woman in the window reflections of the train to and from work. Avey, who chooses to live in suburban North White Plains instead of Brooklyn, is divided not only from her "tribe" but also from herself. Avey's reflection in the mirror is symbolically a reference to how she has "mirrored" or appropriated the exact hegemonic image she resists.

Marshall points to Avey's need to shift from Eurocentric influences to Afrocentric values that move toward black female consciousness to repair her "cultural displacement." Pointing out Avey's all-consuming occupation with whiteness, DeLamotte writes, "Not only is the white culture of consumption starving Avey with its empty excess; it is trying to fill its 'hollowness' by consuming *her* through the process whereby she consumes *it*" (92). The image of whiteness devouring her occurs when Avey decides to take needed time alone. For example, each time on the cruise she tries to find her own space to recover from being around whites, she is overcome with white passengers infringing on her space and mind. "It was always a small mob, who came barging in, bringing in with them their voices.... 'You don't mind if we park near you, do you? Hope we're not disturbing you. Isn't this a great spot!...Is this your first cruise?'" (Marshall 54).

The stimulation from white voices is too much for Avey. "The image of white culture seeking out Avey to devour her by implicating her in its consumption is a literalized image of the danger of assimilation, in which consuming and being consumed are identical" (DeLamotte *Places* 92). The years of acculturating white values—materiality obsession—catches up to Avey as she tries to pull herself away from white culture. The idea of white consumption is further exploited by Marshall in the image of the white passengers' constantly annoying Avey:

> The voices that shattered her brief peace, that seemed determined to draw her down into the hollowness of their talk, to make her part of it, began to have a familiar ring. They sought to escape the last place she had been, as well as the place before that. Even their flushed and suntanned faces struck her as being suspiciously familiar. (Marshall 55)

Avey is overloaded with white ideas and influences and is close to a spiritual breakdown as she moves further away from her true black identity.

A stripping away of superimposed whiteness is necessary for Avey to recover what was lost in the years of consuming whiteness[6] and materiality. Evidence of Avey's need to remove Western cultural influences is clear in the third section of the novel. As a marker of the beginning of Avey's transformation, Marshall places Avey in a dream that suggests the idea of removing or stripping away all that taints Avey's spirituality and wholeness. Having decided to abandon the cruise on the *Bianca Pride*, Avey wakes after a nightmare that makes Avey realize she needs to change:

> In a final turn of her sleep she smelled it. An odor faint but familiar. Somewhere a baby needed changing. It hadn't soiled itself or even wet the diaper.... And it had been left lying in the same cotton kimono for too long...and had begun to smell. *It needed to be stripped,* given a sponge off, then patted dry, oiled and freshly powdered. (*emphasis added*) (149)

The dream symbolizes Avey's need to "strip" or remove the whiteness that separates her from her true self. The dream also represents what Avey has lost along the way in breaking from her ancestral and African roots.

Willis also analyzes what Avey's stripping and purging means during the time she aborts her cruise:

> Avey is stripped of all possessions that previously defined her middle-class life and values—the clothes, the coiffure, and finally the food.... The purge represents a symbolic break from bourgeois consumption and the transition to a very different relationship to food, defined not as a personal indulgence but as an object that articulates communal social relationships. (62)

In this sense, Avey's physical body is preparing for the return to her spiritual wholeness as a black woman. The process toward psyche restoration and female transformation is furthered by Marshall pointing to the requirement of removing remnants of whiteness for the completion of Avey's recovery.

Locations for Holistic Healing

Pettis has pointed out that although some African American women writers address in their fiction the "schism that occurs when blacks—particularly women—ignore the politics (and lessons) of race, class, and gender blindly subscribe to the American dream," Marshall addresses the question of "how African-Americans can remain culturally moored and psychologically whole while participating in economic enterprises that almost guarantee fragmentation" (115). However, this discussion endeavors to extend Pettis's point that Marshall is one of the few black women writers discussing how black women can remain whole while in hegemonic locations. Marshall more interestingly demonstrates the location from which black women recreate themselves as spiritual and whole subjects. In order for women to realize black female transformation for black female reality, Marshall shows what space African American women must inhabit in order to value and identify themselves more holistically.

Avey begins her journey to female wholeness, as mentioned, after dreaming of old Aunt Cuney. When the dream stops, Avey is awakened from her state of unconsciousness when Aunt Cuney, in a vision, implores Avey to take her hand and come with her. Aunt Cuney beseeches Avey to connect with her and her ancestral history to reinstate what she has lost during her climb to middle-class status. "Aunt Cuney's intrusive and disruptive reentry into Avey's comfortable life [although Aunt Cuney is dead] is intended to metaphorically reposition Avey along the path to Ibo Landing from which she has severely strayed" (Pettis 121). As Avey's ancestor, she is the means by which Avey is awakened from her identity collapse from materiality. However, in her determination to remain fixed in her misguided view of living, Avey defies Aunt Cuney's invitation to return. "The old woman continued to wave her forward. . . . She kept up the patient summons; and from where she stood on the unpaved country road, Avey Johnson ignored it, growing more annoyed each time the hand beckoned" (Marshall 41). Aunt Cuney's signaling—"Her hands . . . coaxing her forward . . . urging her . . . [with] " *'Come/O will you come?'* " (41)—initiates Avey on the journey to recovery of her past. As Pettis points out about Avey's dreams, "the ancestral interference precipitates dreams, flashback, and journeys that cumulatively bring Avey to realize her fractured psyche" (121). The importance of Aunt

Cuney in her dreams is that she helps realign Avey with her natural state of identity.

Several past literal voyages encourage Avey's symbolic return from a fractured self to "spiritual wholeness." The first of these journeys begins in Avey's childhood when she travels from the North to the South (from New York to the sea island town of Tatem, South Carolina). Through the lesson of the Ibos, Aunt Cuney tries to instill the importance of keeping distant "a hostile culture"—the hegemony—from her psyche or black female self. In essence, Aunt Cuney, through her lesson of the Ibos to Avey, prepares her for the journey she makes from the time of her aborted ocean cruise, "an exercise in middle-class leisure and luxury," to her regeneration in Carriacou through the living ancestor Lebert Joseph.

Avey's next journey is from the hotel in Grenada to meeting Lebert Joseph in his place of business. Figuratively, Lebert's business is recovering lost souls such as Avey and pointing them back to their African roots and spiritualness. Without Avey telling him more of how she arrived at his place, Lebert with his penetrating look "marked him as someone who possessed ways of seeing that went beyond mere sight and ways of knowing that outstripped ordinary intelligence (*Li gain connaissance*) and thus had no need for words" (172). Lebert, like the Ibos, has special powers of seeing, knowing, and feeling things without others telling him.

Through Lebert, Marshall shows the importance of Avey's journey to Grenada and Carriacou as part of Avey's transformation and reconnection to her ancestral roots and past. Lebert, from his gift that enables to see others' pain and loss, comforts her:

> "You're not the only one, oui.…It have quite a few like you. People who can't tell their nation. For one reason or another they just don't know. Is a hard thing. I don' even like to think about it. But you comes across them all the time here in Grenada. You ask people in this place what nation they is and they look at you like you's a madman. No, you's not the only one." (174–177)

Here, Lebert explains to Avey that there are blacks like her who are disconnected from their past.

In her novel, Marshall examines the point of entering women-centered places for renewal, which is a concern of black women writers in recovering the fragmented self. Black feminist critic hooks describes her desire, when she wrote her first book in knowing whether the oppressed can recover "a wholeness of being" that existed before oppression (*Talking Back* 31). Marshall shows the possibilities for black restoration through Avey in the process of her recovering from her dissociation with her personal and ancestral past. Through discovery and helping women to understand the elements of recovering a connection to self and community, hooks makes the point that blacks must Unlearn the white understanding of "self" as unitary and isolated, recognizing the term instead

> not as signifier of one "I" but the coming together of many "I's," the self as embodying collective reality past and present, family and community. Social construction of the self in relation would mean, then, that we would know the voices that speak in and to us from the past, that would be in touch with…our history. Yet it is precisely these voices that are silenced, suppressed, when we are dominated. It is this collective voice we struggle to recover. (*Talking* 31)

It is in the coming together and the voices of Aunt Cuney and the women of Grenada and Carriacou that Avey begins to recover her familial connection with the black female self.

The communal space in which "Avey begins to reunify her fragmented self" is what DeLamotte identifies as "that solitary place of self-encounter" (*Places* 97). This communal space is seen through the church "Mother's" voices. The "Mothers" on the boat ride to the island for the celebration remind Avey of the old women from her childhood past: "They were…the presiding mothers of Mount Oliver Baptist…the Mother Caldwells and Mother Powes and Mother Greens" whose "voices propelled the sermon forward each Sunday" and whose "arms reached out" to "the sinners and backsliders" who "made their shame faced cavalry up to the pulpit, it was their exhortations which helped to bring them through" (Marshall 194). From these soothing voices and the women on the boat, Avey is stripped of the distorted values of whiteness that pushed her to abort the cruise and the values that had led her down the wrong path of life.

SPIRITUAL CLEANSING FOR FEMALE TRANSFORMATION

In *Praisesong for the Widow*, the fourth phase of the Transient Woman occurs in Avey's transition before her reentry into the dominant culture's space and in her completion of black female transformation. Symbolically, the voyage to Carriacou is Avey's crossing from hegemonic space to Third Space, a site for renewal and transformation. However, the voyage also signifies the purging of white-centered values and the beginning of the cleansing of Avey's female psyche to prepare her for the cross-over to black female consciousness and her black connection. Overcome by seasickness, Avey undergoes a purge, first through a violent attack of vomiting and then, an equally violent bout of diarrhea. Significantly, the purging occurs onboard the boat to Carriacou, and with the help of the "Mothers." In thinking about the unclear happenings for her in the last day, Avey is assured that she is in the right place and time:

> She felt her elderly neighbors on the bench turn toward her. A quieting hand came to rest on her arm and they both began speaking to her in Patois—soothing, lilting words full of maternal solitude...[,] their murmurous voices now set about divesting her of the troubling thoughts, quietly and deftly stripping her of them as if they were so many layers of winter clothing she had mistakenly put on for the excursion. (197)

The women on the boat, the sermon, and the murmured "bon" chorus (in the image of call and response) help Avey to release her past through literally purging of food from her body. As Willis points out,

> the purge represents a symbolic break from bourgeois con-sumption and the transition to a very different relationship to food, defined not as personal indulgence but as an object that articulates communal social relationships. On board the cruise ship, food, all of it heavy and rich, represented decadence,

overabundance, and the impossibilities of ever attaining individual satisfaction. (62)

Recalling the voices discussed earlier by hooks, these voices help Avey feel secure and prepare her for the next stage of spiritual cleansing. These voices are rooted in blackness, the voices that Avey recalled growing up as a black female.

Another voice is recalled by Avey in her trip to Carriacou. Avey recalls a sermon from her childhood in which the preacher delivers the tale of Christ's resurrection in black vernacular English. His "strangled scream, stolen from some blues singer" helps his performance and facilitates obtaining the congregation's response (Marshall 199). Avey recalls the preacher's demand for the church to purge themselves of "stones of sin" and soon after rids herself of the figurative strangling of materiality on her life through actual purging of food from her body. The food in this sense is an image of materialism and whiteness that Avey has consumed over her life and now is being called to purge from the memory of the preacher's sermon. She recalls vividly the preacher's emphasis on values: "There's the shameful stone of false values, of gimme, gimme, gimme and more more more" (201). Avey is reminded of her past and the need to rid herself of values that contaminate her inner being.

Another step in Avey's progression toward spiritual wholeness, the literal cleansing of the body, is performed by Lebert Joseph's daughter, Rosalie Parvay. Implicit in Avey's recovery of her connection with her black female self and black roots is the relationship between place and women who help Avey in her transformation. The narrator notably describes the surroundings in which Rosalie will perform the ritual of cleaning Avey's physical body. The room in Rosalie's house is "large, high-ceilinged and plain, with a bare wooden floor, bare walls[7] and curtainless windows that suggested it was seldom used....And it was sparsely furnished" (215). Marshall's depiction of a "bare room" exemplifies the state from which Avey must recover her female wholeness. She must be stripped of all that defines white cultural values.

Rosalie cleanses Avey's body of remnants of her past life in materiality and false values. In a sense, Avey is placed in an infant-like state in order to return her to innocence. In a motherly fashion, Rosalie tells Avey, "'Come, oui,…is time now to have your skin bathe. And this time I gon' give you a proper wash down'" (217). This proper wash down or the "'laying of hands,'" (217) to which Rosalie refers is a cleansing that must be performed by another who has spiritual and female connection with Avey. In this ritual of cleansing the physical body, Avey gives "herself over then to the musing voice and to such simple matters" as she prepares to cross over to her ancestral and black roots (221).

After bathing Avey's body "systematically and ceremoniously," Rosalie begins the next part of cleaning and preparing the body for Avey's change. The purification of Avey's body signifies the removal of white consumption. Conceptually, Avey's body here is not literal flesh and bones but rather a symbol of her black spirituality. Rosalie oils and massages Avey's body; through this ritual performance, Marshall returns Avey's body to the sensual quality it had years before. As Rosalie's hands work Avey's "arm, [her] shoulder, [her] breast.…her long legs" (220), the manipulation of Avey's body produces from her "a plainsong or chant" (220) and a "stinging sensation that was both pleasure and pain" (Pettis 128). The ritual of cleansing does more than remove the overload of white values, it also returns Avey to her erotic self.

Rosalie's "laying on hands" in the washing and oiling of Avey's body reflects a cultural tradition of African Americans and black women. This practice, in black women's writing, is used "for reclaiming the spiritual dimension of black female characters" (Pettis 128). An example of this laying on hands occurs in Shange's *For Colored Girls* and in Toni Cade Bambara's *The Salt Eaters*, which similarly features the redemption of main character Velma Henry. The revitalizing of Avey's flesh is a requirement and signals Avey's readiness for the crossover and initiation in the ceremony later with Lebert Joseph.

Before the ceremony, Marshall shows Avey's links to her African American and West Indian roots. Her African American roots may have been with "the presiding mothers of Mount Oliver Baptist Church (her own mother's church long ago)" (Marshall 194). The crowd on the Grenada wharf taking the excursion to Carriacou for the holiday ceremony is Avey's tie to her African connection. Avey makes the association with the West Indians as she watches them enter the boats for the yearly ceremony to their dead ancestors. Avey notes,

> She was feeling more dazed and confused than ever, yet there now seemed to be a small clear space in her mind....[Their] bodies, the colors and sounds, the pageantry of the umbrellas were like frames from a home movie she remembered Marion had made on her last trip to Ghana. (187)

Like a family movie, the movement, the colors, and the noises from the people refresh Avey's connection with her past. Moreover, the scene recalls something tangible and rich in her life. Though she is not entirely sure what she is recalling, Avey knows that being with the people reminds her of something important.

Later, in the ceremony presided over by Lebert in Carriacou, Avey's spiritual, literal, and social links between her African American and African roots are brought together. Through Lebert's disappointment with his American grandchildren's lack of African roots, Marshall shows that both African and African American roots are interconnected and necessary for transformation and survival. Lebert, the link to the past and the present, is Avey's tie to her past and present. He is Avey's life bridge for her survival when she returns home in the United States.

The culmination of Avey's transformation occurs in the ceremonial festivities. This change takes place in the proper and natural setting of African roots—on bare earth. The ceremony is a combination of chanting half-remembered names and West African practices such as call-and-response songs to honor family names, and the circular dance accompanied by rum keg drums. Avey watches in curiosity but does not participate. When an old woman makes her entry into the ceremony, Avey's feels that her great-aunt is standing there pushing her to participate in the dance.

Dance in this world has several meanings. Dancing in a circular motion means continuity. Here, it denotes Avey's continuing her connections in West Indian, African, and African American roots. Pettis notes, "Avey's participation in the circular of ancestral reverence resounds with connective significance both for her personally and for the meaning of the novel" (131). As Avey watches from the sidelines, the calling of the nations in dance draws her into the spiritual reawakening of her African roots. She feels the drumming, the dancing, and the humming of the voices somehow right. From within her half-empty mind, following her natural, metaphorical, and ritual purging and cleansing of body and mind, Avey is filled with new thoughts—a feeling of her connections with those who have passed. Pettis cites Franz Fanon's view of the sacred ceremonial circular dance: "As a permissive circle…it protects and permits.…[It reflects] the huge effort of a community to exorcise itself, to liberate itself, to explain itself" (131). In this sense, Avey's transformation is occurring as she renews her ancestral connection to the present.

Performing the Carriacou Tramp is instinctive to Avey. She had seen it danced before, standing with Aunt Cuney in Tatem on the sidelines while the Tatem elders performed. Describing the drums and spirit that overtake the dancers, Marshall shows how Avey's entry into the dance is her step toward realization of her transformation: "She too moved—a single declarative step forward.…And she found herself walking amid the elderly folk on the periphery" (Marshall 247). Avey's dance or stepping on the edge of the circle shows her continuing her family lineage in unison with the dancers of African and West Indian origins. Rosalie is surprised that Avey is doing the Carriacou Tramp, but Avey's smile speaks and shows more than her performance. Avey's grin points to her confidence and the natural state to which she is returning in her performance of the dance she had only observed before with Aunt Cuney. Moreover Avey's naturalness and ease in performing the Carriacou Tramp suggest Avey's spiritual retention of African practices in Southern culture.

Having performed in ceremony, Avey is reborn, a woman "confirmed in her displaced African culture" (Pettis 132). Avey has finally "after all these decades made it across" (Marshall 248). In this sense, her materialistic yearnings and self-disavowal are dead. Avey recovers and reconnects with her ancestral past—the part relative to her wholeness as a black woman in self-understanding and survival.

Like Janie Crawford in *Their Eyes Were Watching God*, Avey returns to her community as a whole subject. Using her daughter Marion in the same way Janie calls on Phoeby in initiating the telling of her story, Avey "would enlist Marion in her cause....Marion alone would understand about the excursion and help her spread the word" (Marshall 255). Comfortable with who she is and where she has come from, Avey confirms herself as a black woman connected with her self outside the ideas of others. Avey learns the lesson from Aunt Cuney—the woman whose name she bore: "Her body she always usta say might be in Tantem but her mind, her mind was long gone with the Ibos" (254–255).

Marshall's cautionary novel offers one way to survive in a materialistic society: through self-acceptance and a changed consciousness that connects black females to their roots in hegemonic spaces that attempt to render them invisible and valueless. She shows in *Praisesong for the Widow* how upward mobility and materialism create tension and the need for the black female subject to shift from Eurocentric cultural values to black-centered values that connect with black female wholeness. For Avey Johnson, black female consciousness and identity are realized when she journeys outside the borders of the United States and her accepted ways of thinking. After seeing her old great-aunt in her dream, Avey moves forward with the same wholeness that has sustained black women in their survival. As Washington writes, "black women who struggle to 'forge an identity larger than the one society would force upon them . . . are aware and conscious, and that very consciousness is portent'" (qtd. in DeLamotte 119). The power of Avey's consciousness is the one encouraged by Aunt Cuney in the act of remembering and resurrecting the black female self from the margins of hegemony's locations.

6

Space and Time: The Interdependency of History, Identity, and Survival in Octavia Butler's *Kindred*

"She dead?"

—Alice in *Kindred*[1]

History is supposed to give people a sense of identity, a feeling for who they were, who they are, and how far they have come. It should act as a springboard for the future. One hopes that it will do this for black women, who have been given more myth than history.

—Deborah Gray White[2]

Nepantleras are the supreme border crossers.

—Gloria E. Anzaldua[3]

In the above passage from *Ar'n't I a Woman*, Deborah Gray White explains the effects of history on a culture and what it provides in terms of those person's uniqueness. According to White, history can also provide the dreams for prosperous futures. In Octavia Butler's *Kindred* (1979), history is treated differently by investigating black women's times past and future through the character Dana Franklin. Hence, in the novel, Butler captures history and its meaning in the context of black women's identity and place. The story is set in 1976— the bicentennial year of the United States—a symbol of America's independence from Britain. As an ironic counterpoint to the celebratory commemoration of United States freed, Butler writes a time-travel novel of African American enslavement in the nineteenth century. *Kindred* reveals Butler's commentary on history and its relationship to the present, particularly in terms of race, class, and gender. Butler's concerns focus on race identity and its implications for black women, their positions in the past, and the relevance of race for the present society as a whole. Within the context of place, Butler weaves a "grim fantasy" (Crossley xii) about the meaning of black female history and a black woman's persistence in saving her history and existence from extinction. The story, as well, portrays the violence imposed on a black woman and her fight to remain intact even when history and time persist in her extinction. The personal and public histories of Butler's Dana in particular are largely influenced by the emotional, psychological, and cultural effects of slavery. This is explicitly clear in Dana's travels between two like cultures and times—Antebellum South and modern-day America. Indeed, Butler brings together these elements to analyze their effects on Dana and her husband Kevin in both nineteenth- and twentieth-century America. The novel is not only about the effects of societal conflicts on Dana, however, but also, more vividly, a commentary on the literal and figurative process of saving black women's history and existence, something this female character must, by necessity, be engaged in.

"SUPREME BORDER CROSSERS"

In understanding the significance of crossings in Butler's *Kindred,* Gloria Anzaldua's idea of nepantlera helps in contextualizing the character Dana's psychological and metaphorical transformation in crossing to "in-between" space of change. In the move across borders and even boundaries of difference, Dana fits the idea of what Anzaldua describes as nepantlera. Dana is positioned as a black woman who exists in two cultures and times that are simultaneously alike and different. As nepantlera, a "supreme border crosser," Dana performs as a black woman in the nineteenth and twentieth centuries—both freedom and enslaved. In modern times, she is defined as free and yet enslaved by hegemonic cultural and oppressive practices. Anzaldua writes,

> Nepantleras are the supreme border crossers. They act as intermediaries between cultures and their various versions of reality. They can work from multiple locations, can circumvent polarizing binaries.... They try to overturn the destructive perceptions of the world that we've been taught by our various cultures. They change the stories about who we are and about our behavior.... They serve as agents of awakening, inspire and challenge others to deeper awareness, greater conocimiento, serve as reminders of each other's search for wholeness of being. ("Speaking Across the Divine" 20)

The idea of nepantleras appropriately fits into this discussion in showing the link between African American and Chicano women as border crossers of difference. African American woman, as Transient Women, are "supreme border crossers" illuminating vividly their efforts toward "female wholeness of being."

BLACK WOMEN'S HISTORY AND SLAVE NARRATIVES

In *Kindred,* a neo-slave narrative,[4] Butler points to the history of African American women and their insistence upon surviving in a society that does not recognize the legitimacy of their existence. Such an example is ex-slave Mary Prince. The idea of writing her history is made clear by Prince herself. "She wished it to be done" so the American public could hear from a slave woman of the physical and sexual abuse she experienced at the hands of her white masters (Ferguson 55). Likewise, former slave Old Elizabeth wished to tell her story from her own perspective, and so it "was taken mainly from her own lips" (*Memoir or Old Elizabeth* in *Six Women's Narratives* 3). Harriet Jacobs, in writing her own history, also "desire[d] to arouse the women of the North to a realizing sense of the condition of two millions women at the South" (1) in testament to black female abuse. Thus, in spite of African American women's historical cultural oppression, they persisted and believed that their gender and race-specific life stories could be best passed on from their own voices and not from the mouths of others.

To make Dana's story a factual record of female slavery and experiences, Butler uses authentic slave accounts and actual sites in her novel. Drawing on examples of black women's abuse, Butler includes in her story the history of sexual exploitation by white men. She focuses attention on Dana's ancestral history as connected with Rufus in exposing the forced sexual relation between Dana's great-grandmother Alice Greenwood and her white great-grandfather Rufus Weylin. The pressures and restrictions of being black and female in the nineteenth century rise to the surface in Butler's story and shows that they are remarkably different from those for black men.

While black male slave narratives are thematically centered on the male narrator's literal escape, African American women's narratives, contrarily, are based on female practices in reconstructing new black female identities. These life stories, thus, point to black women empowering themselves in using their own voices to bring to the American public their own lived experiences as female slaves. Nevertheless, these differences show African American women's commitment to selfhood and point to their being no longer satisfied with identities that defined them as slave and property.

Essentially, female slave narratives disrupt the conventional masculinist slave narrative form. Unlike narratives that show male slave narrators recounting their goal to escape to the North—their typically linear journeys, literally and figuratively— female slave narratives expose sexual abuse to which the narrator herself was subjected. Male slave narratives, as William Andrews reports, generally "would describe the physical torture" (243). However, "the manner in which the sexual abuse of black women was effected, through rape . . . [, it] was deemed too 'disgusting' or 'shocking' to expose to view" (243). Such an instance is in Frederick Douglass's narrative about slave assault. Instead of providing accounts of female sexual abuse he witnessed, Douglass reports only the physical abuse of women.

Female slave narrators, in contrast, recount sexual abuse and other traumatic occurrences, which often open them to scrutiny of a less accepting audience (as in the case of Jacobs). In giving their accounts to abolish slavery, female slaves had double the task in their narratives when revealing the sexual activity between themselves and white slaveholders. Besides writing themselves into existence as persons, they had the burden of redefining themselves as "women" to a white female audience who generally viewed black women as unfit and unworthy.

Female slave narratives embody the tensions from which black women write about their experiences and demonstrate black women's persistence to endure despite the harshness inflicted on them. Elizabeth Keckley, in *Behind the Scenes* (1868), cautiously recounts her sexual abuse and the child to whom she gives birth from the rape by her master. In telling her story to her amanuensis, Sojourner Truth likewise hints at the sexual abuse she experienced as a girl. Olive Gilbert notes how distressful it is for Truth to reveal her sexual mistreatment and writes, "From this source arose a long series of trials in her life of our heroine, which we must pass over in silence; some from motives of delicacy, and others, because the relation of them might inflict undeserved pain on some now living" (*Narrative* 21). In *Incidents*, Jacobs reveals more about her sexual abuse than do her contemporaries and clarifies the anxiety from which she writes in disclosing her sexual history: "I have not exaggerated the wrongs inflicted by Slavery;...I have no motive of secrecy on my own account" (1). In their resistance to being treated indifferently, female slave narrators "define themselves as agents rather that as mere victims, and they record the brutality of their treatment by their owners in order to emphasize their resistance to victimization and their claim to freedom" (Carby 36). Thus, in *Kindred,* her twentieth-century narrative of enslavement, Butler constructs black female voices to expose African American women's hardships and also adds to the earlier nineteenth-century accounts of black women's life experiences.

Significance of Female Slave Narratives with Present

Butler's *Kindred* is a fictitious slave memoir—a writer going back in time—that retells the story of a black woman's ancestral beginnings. As a modern-day black woman and free agent, Dana is still an enslaved woman tied to her nineteenth-century black-white ancestral history. Dana offers a narrative in *Kindred* that encompasses elements from former slaves' narratives. As Foster notes, these slave narratives were "retrospective endeavors which helped the narrators define, even create, their identities as they attempted to relate the patterns and implications of their slavery experiences" (3). Likewise in her account of a nineteenth-century Maryland plantation experience, the character Dana shows how her present-day life in twentieth-century Los Angeles is interlocked with the slave woman Alice Greenwood of 1824. If, as Foster notes, slave narratives are also about former slaves' "efforts to obtain freedom," then for this examination the following questions need to be asked: What is the significance of Dana's efforts in achieving freedom in the nineteenth and twentieth centuries? What does freedom secure for Dana once she returns from her last trip to the past? This examination also looks further at Foster's claim about slave narratives that former slave narrators "attempt to urge the various elements of society to realize their collective need to eliminate injustices and to work for a unity of peace and understanding" (3). In calling for equality, Butler's implicit goal in *Kindred* is to reassess black women's position within hegemonic power by going back in time and space to unfold black women's dilemma in modern society.

The story of *Kindred* centers around the concept of place and time and is full of descriptions of the female protagonist's crossing boundaries of time and space. One of Butler's narrative strategies in the novel is to repeatedly transport Dana across time and space from the antebellum period and 1976. Dana is pulled back in time and space when her slave-owning, white great-grandfather is in trouble and she must save him.[5] However, she is able to return to her present-day existence only when she is in life-threatening danger in the past. That Butler does not spend time discussing the method used to carry Dana back in time and space suggests that she as author is more concerned with "why" the protagonist is moved back to the nineteenth century and what the character gains when she is shifted ahead in the twentieth century. Consequently, as the story unfolds,

Butler sets up the history of slavery and its impact on contemporary blacks and African American women.

With modern-day Dana, Butler recreates life in the nineteenth century for a female slave but with a twist. Using Dana, a black feminist who is educated, cultured, and independent, Butler suggests that African American women demonstrated feminist behavior earlier than that behavior and belief system was ever named. Like former female slaves Truth, Jacobs, and Keckley, Dana is "unruly" and not afraid to take risks when threatened and degraded by the white master and mistress. Dorothy Allison notes that "Dana's attitudes, language, and beliefs about herself are those of black women in 1976. She objects indignantly to being called a 'nigger' by Rufus, is contemptuous of the ignorant white masters" (Allison 475). Though Dana is moved to a time that is radically different from the one in which she developed as a black woman, her resistance to black female oppression remains the same.

Nevertheless, Dana knows when to submit if she is to continue her grandmother's history and to make certain her own future in the twentieth century. Butler reveals in Dana's character her insistence on existing. Dana thinks, "I was careful. As the days passed, I got into the habit of being careful. I played the slave, minded my manners probably more that I had to" (Butler 91). Dana understands when not to contest the master. Like former slaves and by instinct, surviving is a cultivated characteristic for Dana.

The novel reopens the history of slavery, its abuse, and African Americans' skills in survival. Butler's use of travel to slavery's past helps to see slaves as individuals rather than as examples from the distant and disconnected past and sometimes as forgotten persons in history (Crossley xiv). While some see *Kindred* as a narrative form of science and Gothic fiction, the novel is also a historical account of slave abuse. Dana is eyewitness to slave beatings; she comes upon a slave beating by the white nightriders:

> I could literally smell his sweat, hear every ragged breath, every cry, every cut of the whip. I could see his body jerking, convulsing, straining against the rope as his screaming went on and on.

> My stomach heaved, and I had to force myself to stay where I
> was and keep quiet. Why didn't they stop! (Butler 36)

Dana is repulsed by what she witnesses and realizes that if she is
discovered, the same treatment would be certain for her.

Through Dana's travels and experiences to the past, Butler
shows black women's position in antebellum society. African
American slave women worked as many hours as men; they experienced the same beatings as men. On one occasion, Dana is
caught by Rufus's father, Tom Weylin, reading books from his
library, and he beats Dana for disobedience. Dana recounts,

> Weylin dragged me a few feet, then pushed me hard. I fell,
> knocked myself breathless. I never saw where the whip came
> from, never even saw the first blow coming. But it came—like a
> hot iron across my back, burning into me through my light
> shirt, searing my skin,...I screamed, convulsed. (107)

Dana, a learned black woman, is whipped because she is literate.
As a reader she is able to think critically, about the world
beyond—and inside—the plantation; thus she poses a threat to
the illusion of white social order.

Through the lens of time and place, Butler shows the com-
promised positions in which black women are placed by black
and white societies alike. In the present, Dana, as a black
woman, still has to consider what her family and others might
say of her marriage to a white male. Dana confesses to Kevin
that she is "afraid [her] aunt and uncle won't love [him]" and
that her aunt "does not care much for white people, but she
prefers light-skinned blacks" (110, 111). As a "new black
woman" coming out of the radical 1960s in America, Dana
realizes that marriage to a white male is unacceptable. During
her travels to the past, facing a similar reception from whites on
the issue of white-black interrelationships, Dana asserts that
white men could have sexual relationships with black women,
yet African American women were not good enough to marry.

RACE AND GENDER IN THE NINETEENTH
AND TWENTIETH CENTURIES

The novel examines racism and sexism for African American
women through Dana. Butler shows that the issues of race and

gender for black women are the same in the twentieth century as they were in the nineteenth century. Black women are reminded daily of their position and status in hegemonic society. Dana, in 1976, describes her workplace at a "causal labor agency" as "a slave market" (Butler 52). Working for agencies such as the one Dana describes often included working for "minimum wage—minus Uncle Sam's share—for as many hours as you were needed" (52). Work for unskilled blacks in the twentieth century meant

> swe[eping] floors, stuff[ing] envelopes, tak[ing] inventory, wash[ing] dishes, sort[ing] potato chips (really!), clean[ing] toilets, mark[ing] prices on merchandise . . . [,] mindless work, and as far as most employers were concerned, it was done by mindless people. (53)

Like Harriet Jacobs, Dana does the work, "sle[eps] for a few hours," and then gets up "at one or two in the morning" to write (Butler 52). In slavery, men and women used the little time they had for themselves to make a home for their family or, like Dana, to seek literacy as a bold move toward freedom and autonomy. Literacy, in Butler's novel, becomes a liberatory tool to escape white oppression. To ensure a better life in the twentieth century, Dana composes novels. And in the nineteenth century, she writes "passes" for freedom from the Weylin plantation.

Providing an example of the work performed at the "causal labor agency," Butler illustrates why Dana and other blacks try to move from their subservient positions. In *Behind the Scenes*, former slave Elizabeth Keckley describes her efforts to improve her status and save her aged mother from hard labor. She recounts,

> My mother, my poor aged mother, go among strangers to toil for a living! No a thousand times no! I would rather work my fingers to the bone, bend over my sewing till the film of blindness gathered in my eyes; nay, even beg from street to street. (Keckley 45)

In the same way that Dana continues to work even past exhaustion, Keckley understands that to change her situation and status as former slave, she must work harder to advance herself socially and economically as a black woman. As another example of female slaves trying to change their place in society, Jacobs's grandmother "went to work with renewed energy, trusting in time to be able to purchase some of her children" (6). She prepared and sold "crackers, cakes, and preserves" during long hours after working in the white master's house and ultimately "la[id] up three hundred dollars" (Jacobs 6). Endeavoring to take control of their lives through self-determination, black women demonstrate their resistance to white domination.

Butler shows the efforts of one black woman to secure new career choices in the face of opposition to the old guard. At a time when career opportunities are opening for African American females, Dana's aunt and uncle insist that she take a career that serves others. Dana remembers that "after a while, I convinced myself that my aunt and uncle were right....They didn't think of accounting...But they would have approved of it. It's what they would call sensible. They wanted me to be a nurse, a secretary, or a teacher like my mother. At the very best, a teacher" (Butler 55). Dana wanted to be a writer, but her aunt and uncle did not approve of writing as a sensible career for a black female since literacy was conventionally held for whites and males. Dana recalls, "My aunt and uncle said I could write in my spare time if I wanted to,.... Meanwhile, for the real future, I was to take something sensible in school if I expected them to support me" (56). Like the dominant society, blacks are also at fault in consigning African American women to passive positions that do not allow for self-rule.

Yet, Dana learns from her aunt and uncle to be self-sufficient and not indebted to others, a spirit of independence promoted by Maria W. Stewart in her call for black women to "possess the same spirit as men" (38). To Stewart, the power of independence was necessary for black women's survival. Dana understands freedom as self-sufficiency and recalls,

> The independence the agency gave me was shaky, but it was real. It would hold me together until my novel was finished....When that time came, I could walk away...not owing anybody. My memory of my aunt and uncle told me that even people who loved me could demand more of me than I could give—and

expect their demands to be met simply because I owed them. (Butler 109)

Later, Dana forgets her aunt and uncle's advice about not putting the demands of others before her own needs. In marriage, Dana is lost in believing that her independence could remain intact and that "things would be different" with Kevin (109).

Dana's marriage to Kevin dramatizes that her relationship falls into the pattern of male dominance and suggests as well "an uncanny synonymy of the words 'husband' and 'master'" (Crossley xix). Before Dana marries Kevin, he hints at what her position as his wife will consist of: "'Yeah, don't you want to marry me?' He grinned. 'I'd let you type all my manuscripts'" (Butler 109). Even before the marriage, Kevin shows that he expects service. When Dana refuses on several occasions to type his work, Kevin shows the other side of his personality and acts annoyed and angry with Dana's insubordination. Kevin's dual role as white male and spouse can be read as oppressive in the context of his exploitation and objectification of Dana as servant rather than as equal partner in marriage.

Butler demonstrates that marriage for Dana occasionally becomes a hindrance to her selfhood by placing her in a submissive position to her white husband. When Kevin and Dana are on the Weylin's nineteenth-century plantation, they act in the roles of master and slave. Dana is subjected to acting as "whore" and "slave" to her legal husband. Dana thinks, "Somehow, that disturbed me. I felt almost as though I really was doing something shameful, happily playing whore for my supposed owner [Kevin]. I went away feeling uncomfortable, vaguely ashamed" (97). Dana is troubled by what is happening between them and how easily they seemed to have adapted to the situation. For Kevin, it is different and in some ways comfortable to act out the role of master over Dana, as it is familiar and expected in the white household. He even declares that being on the Weylin plantation is a great way to live. In this manner, Kevin fits the white, male, Southern routines far too easily, rather than acting as Dana's partner and protector.

By all indications, Butler is concerned with the positions of African American women in twentieth-century America as explored through Dana who exists as a black female in the nineteenth and twentieth centuries. Though black women are advancing in the workplace and marrying across race lines, there is still the problem of black women acting as "new mammies" of the world and in the work place. As new mammies of the twentieth century, African American women are still burdened with providing for others. In the workplace, black women managers are supposed "to fix systems which are in crisis due to underfunding, infrastructure...[, and] demoralized staff" (Collins 65). According to Nanny in *Their Eyes*, " 'Dat's one of de hold-backs of slavery' " (Hurston 15).

Dana, in modern America, still serves and performs for white superiors, including her white spouse. On the Weylin plantation around 1805, Dana serves and caters to Rufus: Dana "is obliged to become Rufus Weylin's secretary and handle his correspondence and bills" (Crossley xix). Here, Dana's role in the novel is to resolve matters for Rufus, who is emblematic of white power, in order to preserve her own history and identity in the future. Thus, Dana becomes what Collins defines as the "new mammy" figure both in nineteenth and twentieth centuries. What remains to be answered is Butler's motive in portraying her in this manner and whether this portrayal promotes Dana's efforts in recovering her history. As Lorde reminds us,

> The oppressors maintain their position and evade responsibility for their own actions. There is a constant drain of energy which might be better used in redefining ourselves and devising realistic scenarios for altering the present and constructing the future. (115)

Black Women's History Recovered

Survival articulates the power of the African American woman to safeguard black women's history and the protagonist's determination to safeguard her future in the twentieth century. Through Rufus and Hagar Weylin, Dana is able to trace her family history to 1831. Dana realizes that Rufus is part of the link to her past and so she must keep both the man and woman alive. Dana thinks,

> I looked over at the boy who would be Hagar's father. There was nothing in him that reminded me of any of my relatives. Looking at him confused me. But he had to be the one. There had to be some kind of reason for the link he and I seemed to have.... What we had was something new, something that didn't even have a name. Some matching strangeness in us that may or may not have come from our being related. Still, now I had a special reason for being glad I had been able to save him. After all ... after all, what would have happened to me, to my mother's family if I hadn't saved him? (Butler 29)

Butler implicitly reveals the interconnection and interdependency between African Americans and whites despite the racial lines that keep them apart. In fact, the novel's title is synonymous with family and, interestingly, with race. In retrospect, the novel reveals that it is not race that divides African Americans and whites, it is rather blacks' and whites' refusal to recognize that they are more connected than separated. Dana considers the importance of family and keeping both her personal and family histories alive. Butler shows this through Dana's thinking: "Was that why I was here? Not only to insure the survival of one accident-prone small boy, but to insure my family's survival, my own birth.... No matter what I did, he would have to survive to father Hagar, or I could not exist" (29). Family survival figuratively denotes the survival of black and white Americans. Even as Dana considers not helping her slaveholding great-grandfather, she understands that if the young Rufus does not continue to exist, then she will not live in the twentieth century. She responds by helping Rufus and continuing her legacy when she sees how indifference destroys: "But this child needed special care. If I was to live, if others were to live, he must live. I didn't dare test the paradox" (29). Dana realizes that any likelihood of surviving depended on changing her perceptions about whites.

African American women's history shows black women surviving and thriving and proving that they are "not inferior in strength and excellence" (Cooper 140) and that they are the same in character as the Transient Women of the past— rebellious and knowledgeable. Besides showing black women raped and beaten in *Kindred*, Butler appropriately points to strong African American women of the past who made it out of slavery. Butler in her story references Sojourner Truth as well as slaves from fiction and nonfiction. In one instance, Butler brings attention to slaves who are determined to survive and secure freedom from white domination. For instance, when Sarah, who oversees Weylin's house, tells Dana to keep quiet about talk of escape and to look at the blacks who are caught and whipped, Dana counters and says she would rather see and talk to "the ones who make it. The ones living in freedom" (145). Butler makes use of liberatory storytelling and incorporates black women's history of going against the grain to survive as subjects having control over their destinies.

Kindred follows the tradition of black women writers in exposing forms of oppression of the black female psyche and in documenting black women's struggles for female autonomy. Similarly, Butler's novel, like other female slave narratives, demonstrates patterns of bondage—a black woman's determination to break from the oppression of slavery and her resistance in not allowing circumstances to dictate her autonomy. When Rufus insists that Dana call him master, Dana refuses, following the example of female slave resistance in Jacobs's *Incidents in the Life of a Slave Girl*. Surely, Jacobs was cognizant and could think that her privileges and opportunities were like those of white females who were free and self-possessed. Yet, despite the restrictions on her as a female slave, Jacobs exercised autonomy when she could. She repudiated the notion of being concubine to Dr. Flint. Instead, she exercised control of her female sexuality in "trading sexual favors for the protection of another white man, Mr. Sands" (Foster 102).

In Butler's story, Dana uses autonomy and control when she risks her life in fighting against Rufus's attempt to control and rape her. At this point, her future existence is not in jeopardy, as her great grandmother "Hagar has been born" (Butler 241). In the spirit of America's Independence Day, "Rufus call[s] [Dana] back [to his time] on July 4" (243), which is ironically close to the day Dana secures her freedom from Rufus. The last offense by Rufus is his attempt at rape, and it is also Dana's final break from oppression. Dana makes a decision and thinks that she "would never be to him what Tess had been to his father—a thing passed around like the whiskey jug at a husking. He wouldn't do that to me or sell me or" (260). Like other female slave narrators, Dana demonstrates her efforts to remain free and oppose Rufus's will to have and to sell her as his property. In so doing, Dana reveals her determination to maintain control of her freewill and ancestral history:

> I could feel the knife in my hand, still slippery with perspiration. A slave was a slave. Anything could be done to her. And Rufus was Rufus—erratic, alternately generous and vicious. I could accept him as my ancestor, my younger brother, my friend, but not as my master, and not as my lover. (260)

Dana has a determined will to remain whole and intact as a black woman. She resists Rufus's control over her body and exerts her autonomy in existing as a free woman.

FUTURE EXISTENCE IN HEGEMONIC SPACE

Kindred does not offer resolution by removing the images of black women bearing the burdens of all or by structuring an identity different from the past. Instead, Butler's novel questions the overlap of the past with the present through its impact on one character, Dana. At the same time, the story's ending does not propose answers for Dana's future in modern society. How will her experiences in the nineteenth century transform her as a black woman in modern-day America? What new role will Dana take in her marriage with Kevin? The novel's ending may indicate correctly that black women's history in dominant society is ongoing and has no end. Indeed, Butler purposely leaves Dana's narrative open, since African American women continue to cross boundaries to spaces that allow for rethinking their past and their future in hegemonic society.

Ambiguously, Butler closes Dana's history by cutting off part of Dana's arm as she reenters space and time in 1976. The removal of her arm suggests that Dana's existence still remains a part of the past even as she moves back into the present and toward the future. In another way, the loss of Dana's arm evokes a symbolic recovery of black women's bodies when she pulls her arm free from the hold of nineteenth-century ideology. To quote Deborah McDowell on black women using the body as an alternative strategy of resistance, the body becomes "the site of black women's subjection and, simultaneously, the route to their agency and liberation, their 'recovery'" (299). Hence, Butler recovers Dana's agency and liberates her on reentry into the hegemonic space of 1976.

Dana's narrative, as Butler writes, carries on the tradition of female slave narratives by black women who tell their own stories of existence as African American women. Furthermore, Butler adds to the tradition of African American women slave narratives by creating a new criterion against which other narratives and testimonies might be judged. That is, female slave narratives and neo-slave narratives are declarative acts in conveying black women's history through the materializations of black women's recreated identities.

Butler, in her story, provides lessons for future Dana Franklins. Notably, Butler's portrayal of Dana in subservient positions in both the nineteenth and twentieth centuries suggests that she is concerned with black women who, like Dana, might forget their early history as marginalized black women. Butler is interested in alerting black women to the real source of their oppression. In this context, Butler addresses twentieth-century African American women outside the Transient Woman model, who might lose sight of the real source of their oppression and become frustrated in trying to change the oppressor rather than depending on their own inner source of power to move from hegemonic control.

Dana overlooks her oppressor who also shows up in the form of white Rufus. Dana, in her delusional thinking, believes that she can change the boy who will become great- grandfather Rufus and keep him from being the same bad-tempered person as his father. Dana considers,

> "But I would help him as best I could. And I would try to keep friendship with him, maybe plant a few ideas in his mind that

would help both me and the people who would be his slaves in
the years to come. I might even be making things easier for
Alice." (Butler 68)

While it might be amiable on Dana's part to think she can change
her "master," the reality is that the righteous thinking she uses in
the twentieth century is inadequate for 1824. At best, Dana could
work on changing her response to Rufus's erratic behavior and
find ways to remove herself from his control.

However, at the novel's close, it is uncertain whether Dana
has learned any significant lessons in her travels to the past. The
Transient Woman, in this situation, would use the Weylin plantation as the "intervening space" of difference to examine how
structures of hegemonic power work in her life, so that she can
create new ways of being in that space for black female transformation. On her final return to the present, Dana's journey to
1976 Maryland to see evidence of Rufus's and Alice's past is an
indication of her inadequate black female state of being. From
this, doubting Dana still needs to feel and see evidence of the
nineteenth-century past to believe the violence against African
Americans, especially her great-grandmother Alice Greenwood.

What has Dana learned from her experiences in the past? Has
she acquired psychological freedom to any appreciable extent by
the end of her story? If Butler presents a plausible conclusion, it
is that Dana has knowledge of the workings of the hegemony
and that she actively intervenes in continuing her history and
existence when domains of power persist in her extinction.
Carby offers an answer regarding black women's understanding
of hegemonic power, contending that "hegemony is never
finally and utterly won but needs to be continually worked on
and reconstructed, as sexual and racial ideologies are crucial
mechanisms in the maintenance of power" (18). For black
women such as Dana, radical black female subjectivity means
locating sites where female wholeness is realized freely outside
the workings of dominant ideologies that insist on black wom-
en's annihilation. Thus, freedom for black women is realized in
the destruction of the hegemonic interpretation of black wom-
en's history and existence and in a counter-hegemonic space
where black female subjectivity is seen.

7

CONCLUSION

Beyond signifies spatial distance, marks progress, promises the future.

—Homi K. Bhabha[1]

Movement or crossing-over is a necessary antidote to the paralysis of oppression and depression.

—Carole Boyce Davies[2]

It is [the mestiza's] reluctance to cross over, to make a hole in the fence and walk across, to cross the river, to take that flying leap into the dark, that drives her to escape, that forces her into the fecund cave of her imagination, where she is cradled in the arms of Coatlicue, who will never let her go. If she doesn't change her ways, she will remain a stone forever. *No hay mas que cambiar.*

—Gloria Anzaldua[3]

That black women have sought safe spaces for black female transformation and subjectivity demonstrates their very necessary moves out of and away from oppressive hierarchies. Patricia Williams makes clear that hegemonic society distances African Americans from themselves, suggesting that by remaining continually in oppressive places, black women are unable to recognize their conditions and effect change. From Larsen's *Quicksand* and Petry's *The Street*, black female protagonists Helga Crane and Lutie Johnson show the realities of black women who perish by not taking flight or fail to understand and negotiate workings of hegemony. Lutie does not recognize in the beginning that the white American Dream is not held for black women. In her quest for the mythic American Dream, she loses herself and her family.

Helga is also blind in her flight from hegemony and remains in places that prevent autonomy. Helga escapes from one bounded location at Naxos to other places and situations that subject her to the same circumstances as before. In the novel, Helga is also sightless in recognizing herself as an independent, attractive, and passionate black woman. Such is the time when she cannot distinguish that she is the woman in Olsen's picture. In this case, she is disengaged from her true self and does not recognize and appreciate the wholesomeness of black female sexuality. Indeed, Helga's bounded black female identity follows the dangers of the entrapment of the black female self within the hegemonic society that judges black women's erotic and sexuality as dangerous and suspicious.

In Hopkins's *Contending Forces*, secured locations of black female support prove the value of safe space for materializing black female consciousness and forming new identities. Hopkins provides contained spaces in Sappho's room, the women's Sewing Circle, and the New Orleans convent; they are places for nurturing, cultivating, and developing new black women. The "in-between" space in Grenada and Carriacou helps in Avey Johnson's transformation during her literal and figurative purging of white excess after she crosses the American borders. Avey's reconnection with her spiritual, communal, and ancestral ties returns her to a wholeness of being different from her once fractured psyche state. Dana Franklin in Butler's *Kindred* moves back and forth in space and time and connects place with recovery in her fight to remain spiritually and physically intact even when history and time persist in her extinction. Dana's literal and symbolic return to hegemonic space in the twentieth century signifies her determination to use "Beyond" space and time as a vehicle to recover her past and link it with her future.

The act of crossing borders to locations that allow for questioning hegemony and for recovering black women's identity reveals that margins are not places for "radical openness and possibility," as hooks proposes (*Yearning* 149). Instead, margins are places of pain and disenfranchisement. As the narratives of enslavement here show, sites of marginality place black women at a disadvantage and allow for their continual devaluation. "Margins are often uncomfortable places," as Peterson reminds us, "as the lives of African American women, past and present, exemplify, they can be sources of horrifying pain [and] generators of unspeakable terrors" (6). Occupying the margin between races, mixed-race Helga Crane is hurt when she realizes that her aunt and others see and promote her as an oddity, an exotic peacock for public gaze. After white Mrs. Chandler talks with Lutie Johnson like a friend, the latter responds in dismay when Mrs. Chandler suddenly acts indifferent toward her when whites appear in their presence. The stories and novels analyzed here demonstrate that resistance is best initiated and politicized in intervening sites of communal black female effort and support.

The Transient Woman model offered here provides the rationale for female transformation and suggests locations where black female subjectivity can be achieved. The model, which resists "monolithism," adds to discussions of space and identity construction by hooks, Chancy, Peterson, and Collins. The Transient Woman paradigm identifies Third Space as a site to which black women can flee and even return[4] the gaze of the "center" or hegemony. In Third Space, the Transient Woman disengages from the dominant culture's definition of the "True Woman," dismantles those borders preventing black female agency, and in the process creates a space that permits black women to take control of their existence. "Space is a social construct," as Massey points out, and it is in space where social relations are constructed that make the difference (12). For black women, social relations also mean having a visible place in society in which they are not subject to others.

Isolation or alienation for female consciousness and transformation is not utopian but shows that in alienation, black women can find strength. In Hopkins's *Contending Forces,* Sappho and Dora "locked the door of Sappho's room to keep out all intruders" (Hopkins 117) and spent hours in isolation solidifying female relationships. The process toward black female subjectivity includes black women identifying with like women. Similarly, the Women's Club provides a contained space for female knowledge and strength. Here, Sappho is free to have direct discourse on questions about black women's virtue relative to "wrongs which [black women] ha[d] unconsciously committed" (149). Without knowledge and female support, black women like Sappho have little hope of transforming their alleged tarnished images. Isolation in black women's circles is not separation from reality, as some might see it. On the contrary, these isolated locations function temporarily as black women's "center," offering them, as Peterson contends,

> greater possibilities of self-expression as well as the potential to effect social change. Yet even in their marginalized positions these women were not purely "outside of" but remained "a part of"; as such they were never fully free from, but remained in tension with, the fixed social and economic male-dominated hierarchies. (18)

Disenfranchised women can have the resilience to break away from hegemonic domains of power for the goal of reinventing themselves. Chiho Nakagawa reports in her dissertation "Looking for the Gaze of Love: Paranoia, Hysteria, and Masochism in the Gothic" (2005) that "a woman in the modern world cannot easily flee the gaze that aims to utilize her, because she lacks discursive space in the symbolic order" (283). I agree with Nakagawa in her assessment of patriarchal power as controlling women's lives. However, in disordering hegemonic domains of power, there is strength in the possibility of women moving out of their places and articulating agency as they reinsert themselves in the symbolic order. The power of hegemony is not so indestructible and "so controlling and so intrusive that escape is almost impossible" (Nakagawa 283). The works of African American women demonstrate prospects of female realization, a scenario that encompasses female transformation and subjectivity.

In putting forth a model for black women's transformation and a paradigm of black women's movement to safe space, I offer a new perspective from which to read female narratives of enslavement, a perspective that opens new ways to interpret the recurring theme and concern for black female realization and transformation. Still, there is room for further investigation into other means of black female resistance and recovery.

A new discussion of the reformed Transient Woman relative to her new state of being, specifically in marriage, is needed following her reentry into society. Collins reminds us that "black women's safe spaces were never meant to be a way of life" (110). I add to Collins' assertion in contending that black female subjectivity is an ongoing process.

In the continuation of the study of space relative to black women's autonomy, an investigation of the restrictions in the institution of marriage on black women's psyche might be an extension of this project as the theme of marriage is prevalent in each of the works studied. The questions referencing female subjectivity in marriage ask the following: How then can the Transient Woman enter into marriage without achieving additional subjugation by the oppression of gender and male domination? Does marriage produce a self-imposed marginalization for women? How is space in marriage negotiated for continuing black female subjectivity and an identity separate from one's spouse? How is self-possession, a process of reclaiming the lost self, continued once the Transient Woman inherits additional identities through marriage?

Since a number of African American women writers include themes of marriage and motherhood in their works, the concept of black women's movement to new consciousness and identity calls for an inquiry regarding black women's psyche and its return to an oppressive state. While this new investigation can be furthered with the works already used here, other works in the black women writers' tradition should be employed in expanding the discussion of the transformed woman within the confines of marriage. In "The Two Offers" (1859), Francis E. W. Harper comments on marriage and the psychological distress suffered by Laura, who thinks marriage is the goal and the center of a woman's existence. Harper contends, "But woman—the true woman—if you would render her happy, needs more than the mere development of her affectional nature" (25). In *Passing,* Larsen raises questions regarding the influence of marriage on Clare Kendry. Clare fits the model of the Transient Woman, as she is aware of the workings of the hegemony in suppressing black women's movement in white society. Clare conveniently passes when it suits her personal need for comfort, as in the Drake Hotel one hot day. Yet, Clare remains in an unfulfilling marriage and loses part of her psychological stability and black female erotic by the end of the novel. Nel's marriage is the beginning of the end of her friendship with Sula in Morrison's *Sula*. Marriage, in this case, limits her connection with other black women, which was her female sustenance earlier. Moreover, Nel's marriage restricts her possible progress toward female development and movement outside the Bottom. In Hurston's *Their Eyes*, Janie understands how marriage places her at a distance from herself and other women. Jody positions Janie on a pedestal in Eatonville and sets off the hostility of the other women, which prevents female support and nurturing. When Janie believes she has discovered male dominance as essential for her well-being and the basics of a good marriage, she endures physical and psychological abuse from Tea Cake, thus returning to an inferior state of being, as in her previous dysfunctional marriages to Killicks and Jody. For Anna in Jewell Parker Rhodes' *Douglass' Women* (2002), marriage places her more at a disadvantage as a woman than she was as a free black woman before marriage to Frederick Douglass. Such works are only a few of the many writings by African American women that can provide a continued discussion of black women's identity, place, and autonomy.

Finally, what can be learned from this examination is the interconnectedness of place, boundaries, oppression, and black female consciousness. Without domination, there is no need to find places to save and reinvent the black female self. However, for African American women in present hegemonic society, places of renewal—figuratively, metaphorically, and psychologically—are essential for black women's survival.

In the context of the Transient Woman's Third Space and Afro-Caribbean women's exile, Chancy reminds us of the value of black women's discovery of locations outside patriarchal or Eurocentric locations:

[Safe space] functions as the language with which to repair the psychic damage of geographic and cultural alienation, provides the base by which to establish self-definition, the net by which to catch and gather Black women as they struggle to recuperate or recognize their ancestral, African heritage in their day-to-day life, and the bridge over which to cross, after having accomplished all of the above, on the long walk home. (22)

Locating places for resistance in Third Space is a possibility for black women to respond to the oppression and domination by those at the center and simultaneously claim their own center. In that space of radical and creative energy, African American women can be transformed and can return "home" as whole subjects.

Notes

1 Introduction: Places, Borders, and Margins—Locating a Black Feminist Model of Interpretation

1. Pauline Hopkins, *Contending Forces* (New York: Oxford UP, 1988) 146.
2. Eugenia C. DeLamotte, *Perils of the Night* (New York: Oxford UP, 1990) 19.
3. bell hooks, *Yearning* (Boston: South End P, 1990) 152.
4. Carla Peterson makes a critical point about marginality in *"Doers of the Word"* in that the ideal of marginality is problematic. Different from hooks's assertion that the margin is a radical space for revisioning, she asserts that "we must be careful not to fetishize positions on the margins as 'pure' spaces of 'radical openness and possibility' but must recognize that 'margins have been both sites of repression and sites of resistance'"(7). While margins might be employed for a point of departure to black female consciousness, I argue that it is not a secure and creative site for constructing new identities and perspectives on black womanhood.
5. My use and definition of consciousness is adopted from Mae Gwendolyn Henderson that "consciousness…is shaped by the social environment. ('Consciousness becomes consciousness only…in the process of social interaction.')" (*Reading Black, Reading Feminist* 118).
6. All movement is not the same. Some movement can be stagnant, without direction or progression. When I use the term "fluid," I am referring to a movement that is deliberate and determined.

2 Black Female Movement: Conceptualizing Places of Consciousness for Black Female Subjectivity

1. Marti Heidegger, "Building, Dwelling, Thinking," *Poetry, Language, Thought* (New York: Harper and Row, 1971) 152–153.

2. Joyce Pettis, *Toward Wholeness in Paule Marshall's Fiction* (Charlottesville: UP of Virginia, 1995) 23.

3. bell hooks, "Choosing the Margin as a Space of Radical Openness," *Yearning: Race, Gender, and Cultural Politics* (Boston: South End P, 1990) 145.

4. Read more on the controlling images and black women's oppression in Patricia Hill Collins' "Mammie, Matriarchs, and Other Controlling Images" in *Black Feminist Thought* (2000).

5. This idea is seen even today in contemporary soap operas. The portrayal of the mammy figure is kept alive in *Young and the Restless* through the character Aunt Mammie, a staple in the wealthy white Abbot family. Since Mrs. Abbot's early departure from the family, Aunt Mammie keeps the family intact. She cooks, cleans, and counsels the Abbots. When their marriages fail and when they need a mother figure to whom they can complain about their own lives, the father John Abbot and his adult children turn to Aunt Mammie. Like female slaves in nineteenth-century fictional works, Aunt Mammie does not have a family unit of a husband or children. As the "mammy" of the Abbot's house, Aunt Mammie's children are Jack and Jill Abbot. When Aunt Mammie's nieces visit her at the Abbots, they call upon her while she tends to her duties in the kitchen. The soap never shows Aunt Mammie as having a private space of her own or any other life independent of the Abbots. The place and space in which Aunt Mammie resides is similar to the one in which female slaves existed: white-centered space. Because of films like *Gone with the Wind* (1939), *Imitation of Life* (1959), and television's soap opera *The Young and the Restless* (1973), the image of the doting mammy is perpetuated by white mass culture.

6. Catherine Clinton, in "Caught in the Web of the Big House," reports that "blacks were reluctant to discuss such matters [about sex], especially with racial and sexual factors inhibiting responses" (24). The article makes the point that even in WPA interviews the race and sex of the interviewer played a major part in the kind of responses received from the interviewee concerning sex between the races or, as in this matter, between master and slave (24). Likewise, former male slaves were hesitant in revealing "his own or his family's encounters with sexual exploitation" in the WPA surveys of former slaves (25).

7. Deborah Gray White shows in "Jezebel and Mammy" that the notion of black women as sensual women started as early as "when Englishmen went to Africa to buy slaves" and "mistook seminudity

for lewdness. Similarly they misinterpreted African cultural traditions, so that polygamy was attributed to the Africans' uncontrolled lust, tribal dances were reduced to the level of orgy and African religions lost the sacredness that had sustained generations of ancestral worshippers" (29).

8. Fulton quotes Alice Walker that African Americans "must as ruthlessly eradicate any desire to be mistress or 'master'" (89); in Janie's abuse by the men in *Their Eyes* comes out the "residuum of the patriarchal slave institution" (88).

9. In her essay "Uses of the Erotic," Lorde explains that the female erotic is not heterosexual erotic or even sexual eroticism. The "erotic" is the life force and resource that, as Lorde explains, "lies in a deeply female and spiritual plane" and provides the power and energy for women to resist oppressive hierarchies (53). The erotic in this sense provides women a space to experience the deepest of feelings and also a location in which women become fully aware who they are in the act of loving themselves.

10. I make this argument in "Zora Neale Hurston's 'The Gilded Six-Bits': A Story of Materialism and Sexism," a paper presented at the National Association of African American Studies National Conference in Baton Rouge, LA, February 11–16, 2008.

11. Domestic violence, in "The Gilded Six-Bits," includes Joe's objectification of Missie May as his possession to own and trade to the highest bidder—Otis Slemmons.

12. In some college classrooms, the perceptions of black women as expressed by white and black students, are surprisingly provocative. In my course "Unruly Voices of African American Women," students have discussed and examined the various stereotypes surrounding black females. Each semester, the list of stereotypes is longer and more offensive. The Jezebel image always appears on the lists, even though students are not entirely certain of its meaning. Nevertheless, by the end of the course, students establish that black women's sexuality is systematically exploited, as in slavery, and is negatively impacted by current mass cultural portrayals of African American women and the black female body. (Class discussion, Instructor Lynette Myles, AFH 394 Unruly Voices of African American Women: Arizona State University, Spring 2004.)

13. It is critical for white feminists and men to understand that it is virtually impossible and unproductive to try and place black women and black men, black feminists and white feminists, blacks and whites in the same box or category and carry on as if

differences do not exist as Bhabha asserts. In an interview about the intervening space of difference and the idea of cultural diversity, he argues that "the assumption that at some level all forms of cultural diversity may be understood on the basis of a particular universal concept, whether it be 'human being,' 'class' or 'race,' can be both very dangerous and very limiting in trying to understand the ways in which cultural practices construct their own systems of meaning and social organization" ("The Third Space" 209). While we can appreciate our differences—men and women, black feminists and white feminists—race and gender differences cannot be evaluated the same way for each group.

14. In chapter 5, I will discuss purging and cleansing for a changed consciousness with Paule Marshall's *Praisesong for the Widow*.

15. Such denial and rejection mark this in the form of "the refusal of the categories of the imperial culture, its aesthetic, its illusory standard of normative or usage, and its assumption of a traditional and fixed meaning 'inscribed in the words'" (Ashcroft, Griffiths, and Tiffin 38).

16. The Transient Woman is a concept I developed during a graduate course on nineteenth-century novels of resistance before learning of Alice Walker's ideas of "The Suspended Woman," "The Assimilated Woman," and "The Emergent Woman." Walker, in her assessment of African American women, sees a black woman's experiences as a series of movements "from a woman totally victimized by society and by men to a growing, developing woman whose consciousness allows her to have some control over her life" (Washington, "Teaching" 212).

17. I am borrowing and modifying Bhabha's "beyond" for use with the Transient Woman notion.

18. Introduced by Walker in *In Search of Our Mothers' Gardens: Womanist Prose* (1983), "womanism" references black women feminism. Walker defines it as "from the black folk expression of mothers to female children, 'You acting womanish,' i.e., like a woman. Usually referring to outrageous, audacious, courageous or *willful* behavior." A womanist is "a woman who loves other women, sexually and/or nonsexually. Appreciates and prefers women's culture, women's emotional flexibility (values tears as natural counter-balance of laughter), and women's strength. Sometimes loves individual men, sexually and/or nonsexually. Committed to survival of wholeness of entire people periodically, for health" (xi).

19. My use of Third Space for the Transient Woman will follow in the discussion of Bhabha.

20. The Transient's Woman stages were developed prior to my knowledge of Anzaldua's model.

21. The problem of the mestiza having two identities and two cultures relates to W. E. B. DuBois's (1903) concept of "double consciousness." The concept refers to African Americans' problems of self-definition while living within a white society, their exclusion from mainstream America and blacks' internal conflicts between what is definitely black and what is American.

22. From a Homi Bhabha interview, "The Third Space" on cultural differences (211).

23. For this study, beyond with a capital B denotes the "Beyond" African American women travel to after moving from the margin or "in-between" space. Bhabha explains the ideal as "the 'beyond' is neither a new horizon, nor a leaving behind of the past.... Beginnings and endings may be the sustaining myths of the middle years; but in the *fin de siècle*, we find ourselves in the moment of transit where space and time cross to produce complex figures of difference and identity, past and present, inside and outside, inclusion and exclusion. For there is a sense of disorientation, a disturbance of direction, in the 'beyond': an exploratory, restless movement caught so well in the French rendition of the words *au-dela*—here and there, on all sides, *fort/da*, hither and thither, back and forth" (*Location* 1). Bhabha extends his definition of what it means to "dwell 'in the beyond.'" He writes that "to dwell in the beyond" also means "to be part of a revisionary time, a return to the present to redescribe our cultural contemporaneity; to reinscribe our human, historic commonality; *to touch the future on its hither side*" (7).

24. In "The Commitment to Theory," Bhabha makes the point and raises questions about the function of critical theory in the context of the assumption by some that that "theory is necessarily the elite language of the socially and culturally privilege" (*The Location of Culture* 19) and "the language of theory is merely another ploy of the culturally privileged Western elite to produce a discourse of the Other that reinforces its own power-knowledge equation" (20–21). While Bhabha's comments on the language of theory is valid, I bring attention to the significance of creating and theorizing black feminist theory for an understanding of the literature as produced by African American women writers. For African American women writers, my study like Homi Bhabha's

"takes the stand on the shifting margins of [social, racial, and] cultural displacement" and demonstrates the function of the theory using the concept of the "Transient Woman" in investigating how black women use specific places of location for black female consciousness. As a rationale in constructing theory relating to female subjectivity, I am reminded of Anzaldua's position on theorizing. In the introduction to *Making Face, Making Soul,* she suggests that it is critical that women of color "occupy theorizing space' and begin reshaping it from within." She further asserts that "theory produces effects that change people and the way they perceive the world. Thus we need *teorias* that will enable us to interpret what happens in the world, that will explain how and why we relate to certain people in specific ways, that will reflect what goes on between…the personal 'I', and the collective 'we' of our ethnic communities" (xxv).

3   LOCATION, FEMALE AUTONOMY, AND IDENTITY IN PAULINE HOPKINS'S *CONTENDING FORCES*

1. Pratibha Parma, qtd. in bell hooks, "Choosing the Margin," *Yearning* (Boston: South End P, 1990) 152.
2. Bhabha, 1–2.
3. I am employing "girlfriend" in the same context as Quashie's description that "the girlfriend is this other someone who makes it possible for a Black female subject to bring more of herself into consideration, to imagine herself in a wild safety" (18).
4. I am emphasizing and using "with" and "as," as per Quashie (16).
5. Davies identifies the politics of location as concepts of place, placement, displacement; location, dislocation; memberment, dismemberment; citizenship, alienness; boundaries, barriers, transportation; peripheries, cores, and centers (153).

4   AT THE CROSSROADS OF BLACK FEMALE AUTONOMY, OR DIGRESSION AS RESISTANCE IN *QUICKSAND* AND *THE STREET*

1. hooks, *Yearning* 148–149.
2. Bhabha, "Third" 211.
3. In the patriarchal society of the nineteenth century, as Barbara Welter explains in her study of the "The Cult of True

Womanhood," a woman had to possess certain virtues that elicit worthiness as characterized for a "True Woman." The characteristics used to judge women as embodiments of "True Womanhood," according to Welter, consisted of four principal virtues: piety, purity, submissiveness, and domesticity. If a woman displayed such virtues, she would have status, wealth, and happiness. However, if she failed to possess such qualities, her chances of marrying or holding a position of status would be nil.

4. This study, following Pettis, defines psyche as the "invisible soul that complements the physical body" and affects identity and personal survival (Pettis 11).

5. A concept continued by Alain Locke during the Harlem Renaissance era that focused on changing American views of African Americans. The idea was to dispel the notion of "old negro" to the idea of "the New Negro," embracing a "new psychology" and "new spirit" that showcased African American accomplishments.

6. The term "reference" here is a reminder of the same treatment that female slave narrators faced when promoting their slave narratives as a record of their lived experiences as slaves. Such narratives were often prefaced with testimonies from whites authenticating the ex-slave's identity and history as a slave.

5 *Praisesong for the Widow*: Crossing Location and Space toward Female Consciousness and Wholeness

1. *Quicksand* 56–57, emphasis added.
2. Marshall, *Praisesong* 226.
3. It is particularly important to note that subjectivity is realized differently for black women in marriage than for whites (male and female) in the nineteenth century. For black women, the very act of choosing their own partner and the act of legally marrying show autonomy in every sense. Marriage under these terms shows black women acting independently in thought and action without the master's choice or consent to mate. Ann duCille, in *The Coupling Convention* (1993), a sentimental novel, confirms the difference relative to black women. On marriage, she says, "But while the marriage plot has been coded as white, female, and European, its relationship to the African American novel has always been highly political. Making unconventional use of conventional literary forms, early black writers appropriated for their own emancipatory

purpose both the genre of the novel and the structure of the marriage plot" (3). duCille notes that black women writers have used the marriage plot as a trope "through which to explore not only so-called more compelling questions of race, racism, and racial identity but complex questions of sexuality and female subjectivity as well" (4).

4. The African and American identities here are similar to the mestiza's identity dualness in living as both Mexican and American.

5. Marshall's text should not be read as too essentialist. The interpretation of how white values and beliefs have an effect on individuals outside white identity is as practical with other racial groups. Anzaldua recognizes the distress caused by hegemonic influences on the Mexican Indian psyche. In her examination of the New Mestiza, she understands that the mestiza is influenced by the American culture and eventually gains an American identity or self when she crosses borderlands. A problem for the New Mestiza is having two identities and the conflict in choosing the cultural identity to which to remain true. To solve her predicament, the New Mestiza, according to Anzaldua, must decide and "learn to juggle cultures" (101). The point here is that other cultures also recognize the influence of Eurocentric values and their psychological affect in the fracturing of individuals' innate cultural identity.

   One may question how likely is it not to be influenced in someway by European beliefs and values if one is black in America. The answer is that it is impossible for blacks, living in white society, to avoid hegemonic influences. However, the dilemma, for blacks, is learning how to exist in dominant society without displacing their innate cultural identity and beliefs. Like the New Mestiza, African Americans must recognize and resolve hegemonic impact and heal through a purging of hegemonic manifestations that create the fractured psyche. Marshall, similar to Larsen who also writes about the fractured psyche of blacks ruptured by materiality, passing, and other such factors, adds to the discussion by providing solutions for preventing disastrous psychological ends for African Americans.

6. Whiteness, in this context, is a dominant ideology as expressed in Eurocentric values and beliefs that denote one's privileged position in hegemonic society.

7. This idea of "bareness" resonated with Sappho's own recovery in the bare room of the New Orleans convent.

6 Space and Time: The Interdependency of History, Identity, and Survival in Octavia Butler's *Kindred*

1. Octavia Butler, *Kindred,* p. 38.
2. Deborah Gray White, *Ar'n't I a Woman?* 3.
3. Gloria E. Anzaldua, "Speaking across the Divide: An Email Interview," p. 20.
4. I use Ashraf H. A. Rushdy's definition of neo-slave narrative in *The Oxford Companion to African American Literature* that describes a neo-slave narrative as "modern or contemporary fictional works substantially concerned with depicting the experience or the effects of New World slavery. Having fictional slave character as narrators, subjects, or ancestral presences, the neo-slave narratives' major unifying feature is that they represent slavery as a historical phenomenon that has lasting cultural meaning and enduring social consequences" (533). This definition serves sufficiently in defining *Kindred* as a neo-slave narrative and explains how Butler uses slavery in her story with the character Dana who navigates between her ancestral slave history in nineteenth-century South and her own sense of slavery in twentieth-century America.
5. Interestingly, Butler reverses the gender-race order in showing black women saving men.

7 Conclusion

1. Bhabha, *Location* 4.
2. Davies, 16.
3. Anzaldua, 71.
4. I use the term "return" purposefully to show African American women's agency in disrupting hegemony power to judge and marginalize their existence.

Bibliography

Allison, Dorothy. "The Future of the Female: Octavia Butler's Mother Lode." *Reading Black, Reading Feminist.* Ed. Henry Louis Gates, Jr. New York: Penguin, 1990. 471–478.

Andrews, William. *To Tell a Free Story*: The First Century of Afro-American Autobiography, 1760–1860. Urbana: U of Illinois P, 1988.

Anzaldua, Gloria. *Borderlands La Frontera.* San Francisco: Aunt Lute Books, 1987.

———, ed. *Making Face, Making Soul/Haciendo Caras: Creative and Critical Perspectives by Women of Color.* San Francisco: Aunt Lute Books, 1990.

———. "Speaking across the Divide: An Email Interview." *SAIL: Studies in American Indian Literatures* 15.3–4 (Fall 2003–Winter 2004): 7–21.

Apgar, Sonia C. "Fighting Back on Paper and in Real Life: Sexual Abuse Narratives and the Creation of Safe Space." *Creating Safe Space: Violence and Women's Writing.* Ed. Tomoko Kuribayashi and Julie Tharp. Albany: State U of New York, 1998. 47–58.

Ashcroft, Bill, Gareth Griffiths, and Helen Tiffin, eds. *The Empire Writes Back. Theory and Practice in Post-colonial Literatures.* London: Routledge, 1989.

Awkward, Michael. *Inspiriting Influences: Tradition, Revision, and Afro-American Women's Novels.* New York: Columbia UP, 1989.

Baker, Houston A. Jr. *Workings of the Spirit: The Poetics of Afro-American Women's Writing.* Chicago: U of Chicago P, 1991.

Bambara, Toni Cade. *The Black Woman.* New York: Simon & Schuster, 1970.

———. *The Salt Eaters.* New York: Random House, 1980.

Bell, Bernard W. "Ann Petry's Demythologizing of American Culture and Afro-American Character." *Conjuring: Black Women, Fiction, and Literary Tradition.* Ed. Marjorie Pyrse and Hortense Spillers. Bloomington: Indiana UP, 1985. 105–115.

Berlin, Ira, Steven F. Miller, and Leslie S. Rowland. "Afro-American Families in the Transition from Slavery to Freedom." *Black Women in United States History*. 4 vols. Ed. Darlene Clark Hine. Brooklyn: Carlson, 1990. 85–121.

Bhabha, Homi K. "Cultural Diversity and Cultural Differences." *The Post-colonial Studies Reader*. Ed. Bill Ashcroft, Gareth Griffiths, and Helen Tiffin. London: Routledge, 1995. 206–209.

———. "Postcolonial Criticism." *Redrawing the Boundaries*. Ed. Stephen Greenblatt and Giles Gunn. New York: MLA, 1992. 437–465.

———. *The Location of Culture*. London: Routledge, 1994.

———. "The Third Space: Interview with Homi Bhabha." *Identity: Community, Culture, Difference*. Ed. Jonathan Rutherford. London: Lawrence and Wishart, 1990. 207–221.

Bone, Robert A. *The Negro Novel in America*. New Haven: Yale UP, 1965.

Brooks, Kristina. "New Woman, Fallen Woman: The Crisis of Reputation in Turn-of-the-Century Novels by Pauline Hopkins and Edith Wharton." *Legacy* 13 (1996): 91–112.

Butler, Octavia. *Kindred*. Boston: Beacon P, 1979.

Carby, Hazel. *Reconstructing Womanhood: The Emergence of the Afro-American Woman Novelist*. New York: Oxford UP, 1987.

Chancy, Myriam J. A. *Searching for Safe Spaces: Afro-Caribbean Women Writers in Exile*. Philadelphia: Temple UP, 1997.

Christian, Barbara. *Black Women Novelists: The Development of a Tradition, 1892–1976*. Westport, CT: Greenwood P, 1980.

———. "The Race for Theory." *Within the Circle: An Anthology of African American Literary Criticism from the Harlem Renaissance to the Present*. Ed. Angelyn Mitchell. Durham: Duke UP, 1994. 348–359.

———. "Trajectories of Self-definition: Placing Contemporary Afro-American Women's Fiction." *Black Feminist Criticism: Perspectives on Black Women Writers*. Ed. Barbara Christian. New York: Pergamon P, 1985. 171–185.

Collins, Patricia Hill. *Black Feminist Thought: Knowledge, Consciousness, and the Politics of Empowerment*. New York: Routledge, 2000.

Cooper, Anna Julia. *A Voice from the South*. 1892. New York: Oxford UP, 1988.

Corner, Tawana Chimney. Foreword. *Contending Forces*. By Pauline Hopkins. 1900. New York: Oxford UP, 1988. I–III.

Crafts, Hannah. *The Bondwoman's Narrative.* Ed. Henry Louis Gates, Jr. New York: Warner, 2002.

Crossley, Robert. Introduction. *Kindred.* By Octavia Butler. Boston: Beacon P, 1979. ix–xxvii.

Davies, Carole Boyce. *Black Women, Writing and Identity: Migrations of the Subject.* London: Routledge, 1994.

Davis, Thadious M. *Nella Larsen Novelist of the Harlem Renaissance.* Baton Rouge: Louisiana State U P, 1994.

DeLamotte, Eugenia C. *Perils of the Night: A Feminist Study of Nineteenth-Century Gothic.* New York: Oxford UP, 1990.

———. *Places of Silence, Journeys of Freedom.* Philadelphia: U of Pennsylvania P, 1998.

Douglass, Frederick. *Narrative of the Life of Frederick Douglass, an American Slave: Written by Himself,* 1845. New York: Barnes & Noble Classics, 2003.

DuBois, W. E. B. *The Souls of Black Folk.* New York: Vintage, 1990.

DuCille, Ann. *The Coupling Convention: Sex, Text, and Tradition in Black Women's Fiction.* New York: Oxford UP, 1993.

Ethnic Notions. Dir., Prod., Writer Marlon T. Riggs. California Newsreel, 1987.

Ferguson, Moira. Introduction. *The History of Mary Prince.* By Mary Prince. Ann Arbor: U of Michigan P, 1997. 1–51.

Foster, Francis Smith. *Written by Herself: Literary Production by African American Women, 1746–1892.* Bloomington: Indiana UP, 1993.

Fulton, DoVeanna S. *Speaking Power: Black Feminist Orality in Women's Narratives of Slavery.* Albany: State U of New York P, 2006.

Gates, Henry Louis, Jr., ed. *Collected Black Women Narratives.* New York: Oxford UP, 1988.

———, ed. *Reading Black, Reading Feminist: A Critical Anthology.* New York: Meridian, 1990.

———, ed. *Six Women's Slave Narratives.* New York: Oxford UP, 1988.

Giddings, Paula. *When and Where I Enter: The Impact of Black Women on Race and Sex in America.* New York: Bantam Books, 1984.

Gilkes, Cheryl Townsend. "From Slavery to Social Welfare: Racism and the Control of Black Women." *Class, Race, and Sex: The Dynamics of Control.* Ed. Amy Swerdlow and Hanna Lessinger. Boston: G.K. Hall, 1983. 288–300.

Gone With the Wind. Dir. Victor Fleming. Prod. David O. Selznick. Clark Gable, Vivien Leigh, Hattie McDaniel. Metro-Goldwyn-Mayer, 1939.

Green, Renee. In conversation with Donna Harkavy. Curator of Contemporary Art. Worchester Museum.

Griffin, Farah Jasmine. *"Who Set You Flowin'?": The African-American Migration Narrative.* New York: Oxford UP, 1995.

Gwin, Minrose C. *"Jubilee:* The Black Woman's Celebration of Human Community." *Conjuring: Black Women, Fiction and Literary Tradition.* Ed. Marjorie Pryse and Hortense J. Spillers. Bloomington: Indiana UP, 1985. 132–149.

Harper, Frances Ellen Watkins. *Iola Leroy, or Shadows Uplifted.* 1892. *Three Classic African American Novels.* Ed. Henry Louis Gates, Jr. New York: Vintage, 1990. 227–461.

———. "The Two Offers." 1859. *Centers of the Self: Stories by Black American Women from the Nineteenth Century to the Present.* Ed. Judith A. and Martin J. Hamer. New York: Hill and Wang, 1994. 21–30.

Heidegger, Marti. "Building, Dwelling, Thinking." *Poetry, Language, Thought.* New York: Harper and Row, 1971. 152–153.

Henderson, Mae Gwendolyn. "Speaking in Tongues: Dialogics, and the Black Women's Writer's Literary Tradition." *Reading Black, Reading Feminist: A Critical Anthology.* Ed. Henry Louis Gates Jr. New York: Meridian, 1990. 117–142.

Hoeveler, Diane Long. *Gothic Feminism: The Professionalization of Gender from Charlotte Smith to the Brontes.* University Park, PA: Pennsylvania State UP, 1998.

Hoeveler, Diane Long, and Janet K. Boles, eds. *Women of Color: Defining the Issues, Hearing the Voices.* Westport, CT: Greenwood P, 2001.

hooks, bell. *Ain't I a Woman: Black Women and Feminism.* Boston: South End P, 1981.

———. *Sisters of the Yam.* Boston: South End P, 1993.

———. *Talking Back.* Boston: South End P, 1993.

———. *Yearning: Race, Gender, and Cultural Politics.* Boston: South End P, 1990.

Hopkins, Pauline E. *Contending Forces: An Illustrative Romance of Negro Life North and South.* 1900. New York: Oxford UP, 1988.

Hull, Gloria, Patricia Bell-Scott, and Barbara Smith, eds. *All the Women Are White, All the Blacks Are Men, but Some of Us Are Brave.* New York: Feminist P, 1982.

Hurston, Zora Neale. *Their Eyes Were Watching God.* 1937. New York: Harper, 1990.

———. "The Gilded Six-Bits." *Spunk: The Selected Short Stories of Zora Neale Hurston.* New York: Marlowe, 1985. 54–68.

Imitation of Life. Dir. Douglas Sirk. Perf. Lana Turner, Juanita Moore. Universal Pictures, 1959.

Jacobs, Harriet. *Incidents in the Life of a Slave Girl.* 1861. Cambridge, MA: Harvard UP, 1987.

Keckley, Elizabeth. *Behind the Scenes. Or, Thirty Years a Slave, and Four Years in the White House.* 1868. New York: Oxford UP, 1988.

Kuribayashi, Tomoko, and Julie Tharp. *Creating Safe Space: Violence and Women's Writing.* New York: State U of New York P, 1998.

Larsen, Nella. *Quicksand* and *Passing.* 1928. 1929. New Brunswick: Rutgers UP, 1986.

Lorde, Audre. *Sister Outsider: Essays and Speeches by Audre Lorde.* Freedom, CA: Crossing P, 1984.

Marshall, Paule. *Brown Girl, Brownstones.* New York: Feminist Press, 1981.

———. *Praisesong for the Widow.* New York: Plume, 1983.

Massey, Doreen. "New Directions in Space." *Social Relations and Spatial Structure.* Ed. Derek Gregory and John Urry. London: Macmillan, 1985. 9–19.

———, ed. "Space, Place, and Gender." *Space, Place, and Gender.* Cambridge, UK: Polity P, 1994. 175–244.

McCullough, Kate. *Regions of Identity: The Construction of America in Women's Fiction, 1885–1914.* Stanford: Stanford UP, 1999.

Minh-ha, Trinh T. *Woman Native Other: Writing Postcoloniality and Feminism.* Bloomington: Indiana UP, 1989.

Morrison, Toni. *Sula.* New York: Plume, 1982.

Myles, Lynette D. "Zora Neale Hurston's 'The Gilded Six-Bits': A Story of Materialism and Sexism." National Association of African American Studies National Conference. Baton Rouge, LA. 11–16 Feb. 2008.

Nakagawa, Chiho. "Looking for the Gaze of Love: Paranoia, Hysteria, and Masochism in the Gothic." Diss. Arizona State U, 2005.

Painter, Nell Irwin. *Sojourner Truth: A Life, a Symbol.* New York: Norton, 1996.

———. "Truth in Photographs." *Sojourner Truth: A Life, A Symbol.* New York: Norton, 1996. 185–199.

Peterson, Carla L. *"Doers of the Word": African-American Women Speakers and Writers in the North (1830–1890).* New Brunswick: Rutgers UP, 1995.

Petry, Ann. *The Street.* Boston: Beacon P, 1946.

Pettis, Joyce. *Toward Wholeness in Paule Marshall's Fiction.* Charlottesville: UP of Virginia, 1995.

Picquet, Louisa. *Louisa Picquet, The Octoroon*. 1861. *Collected Black Women Narratives*. Ed. Henry Louis Gates, Jr. New York: Oxford UP, 1988. 5–60.

Prince, Mary. *The History of Mary Prince, a West Indian Slave*. 1831. *Six Women's Slave Narratives*. Ed. Henry Louis Gates, Jr. New York: Oxford UP, 1988. 1–44.

Prince, Mary. *The History of Mary Prince, a West Indian Slave*. 1831. Ed. Moira Ferguson. Ann Arbor: U of Michigan P, 1997.

Pryse, Marjorie, and Hortense Spillers, eds. *Conjuring: Black Women, Fiction, and Literary Tradition*. Bloomington: Indiana UP, 1985.

Pryse, Marjorie. "Pattern against the Sky": Deism and Motherhood in Ann Petry's *The Street*. *Conjuring: Black Women, Fiction, and Literary Tradition*. Ed. Marjorie Pryse and Hortense Spillers. Bloomington: Indiana UP, 1985. 116–131.

Quashie, Kevin Everod. *Black Women, Identity, and Cultural Theory*. New Brunswick: Rutgers UP, 2004.

Rhodes, Jewell Parker. *Douglass' Women*. New York: Atria Books, 2002.

Robertson, James O. *American Myth, American Reality*. New York: Hill and Wang, 1980.

Royster, Jacqueline Jones. *Traces of a Stream: Literacy and Social Change among African American Women*. Pittsburgh: U of Pittsburgh P, 1994.

Rushdy, Ashraf H. A. "Neo-slave Narrative." *The Oxford Companion to African American Literature*. Ed. William L. Andrews, Frances Smith Foster, and Trudier Harris. New York: Oxford UP, 1997. 533–535.

Rutherford, Jonathan. "Interview with Homi Bhabha." *Identity: Community, Culture, Difference*. Ed. Jonathan Rutherford. London: Lawrence and Wishart, 1990. 207–221.

Shange, Ntozake. *For Colored Girls Who Have Considered Suicide/When the Rainbow Is Enuf.* New York: Scribner, 1977.

Sonia-Hull, Saldivar. Introduction. *Borderlands: La Frontera: The New Mestiza*. Gloria Anzaldua. San Francisco: Aunt Lute Books, 1987. 1–15.

Stewart, Maria W. "Religion and the Pure Principles of Morality." *America's First Black Woman Political Writer*. Ed. Marilyn Richardson. Bloomington: Indiana UP, 1987. 28–42.

Tate, Claudia. Ed. Introduction. *Black Women Writers at Work*. New York: Continuum, 1983. xv–xxvi.

————, ed. "Alexis DeVeaux." *Black Women Writers at Work*. New York: Continuum, 1983. 49–59.

————. "Desire and Death: Seducing the Lost Father in *Quicksand*, by Nella Larsen." *Psychoanalysis and Black Novels: Desire and the Protocols of Race*. New York: Oxford UP, 1998. 119–147.

————. *Domestic Allegories of Political Desire*. New York: Oxford UP, 1992.

Truth, Sojourner. *Narrative of Sojourner Truth*. 1850. New York: Penguin, 1998.

Turner, Nat. *The Confessions of Nat Turner and Related Documents*. 1831. Ed. Kenneth S. Greenberg. Boston: Bedford, 1996.

Walker, Alice. *In Search of Our Mothers' Gardens: Womanist Prose*. San Diego: Harcourt, 1983.

————. "In Search of Our Mothers' Gardens." *Within the Circle: An Anthology of African American Literary Criticism from the Harlem Renaissance to the Present*. Ed. Angelyn Mitchell. Durham and London: Duke UP, 1994. 402–409.

————. *The Color Purple*. Orlando: Harcourt, 1982.

Weiner, Marli F. *Mistresses and Slaves: Plantation Women in South Carolina, 1830–80*. Urbana: U of Illinois P, 1997.

Welter, Barbara. *Dimity Convictions: The American Woman in the Nineteenth Century*. Columbus: University of Ohio P, 1976.

Washington, Mary Helen. "The Darkened Eye Restored." *Within the Circle*. Ed. Angelyn Mitchell. Durham: Duke UP, 1994. 443–453.

————. "Teaching *Black-Eyed* Susans: An Approach to the Study of Black Women Writers." *All the Women Are White, All the Blacks Are Men, But Some of Us Are Brave*. New York: Feminist Press, 1982. 208–217.

————. Introduction. *Their Eyes Were Watching God*. By Zora Neale Hurston. New York: Harper and Row, 1990.

White, Deborah Grey. *Ar'n't I a Woman? Female Slaves in the Plantation South*. New York: Norton, 1985.

————. "Jezebel and Mammy: The Mythology of Female Slavery." *Ar'n't I a Woman? Female Slaves in the Plantation South*. New York: Norton, 1985. 27–61.

Williams, Patricia J. *The Alchemy of Race and Rights*. Cambridge, MA: Harvard UP, 1991.

Williams, Sherley Anne. *Dessa Rose*. New York: Morrow, 1986.

Willis, Susan. *Specifying: Black Women Writing*. Madison: U of Wisconsin P, 1989.

Wilson, Harriet E. *Our Nig: Or, Sketches from the Life of a Free Black.* 1859. New York: Vintage, 1983.

Winter, Kari J. *Subjects of Slavery, Agents of Change: Women and Power in Gothic Novels and Slave Narratives, 1790–1865.* Athens: U of Georgia P, 1992.

The Young and the Restless. CBS Broadcasting, 1973.

Index

Africa, 41, 133

Agency,
    female, 2, 5, 39, 120, 122
    self, 13, 31, 92, 120–1, 162,
        167–8, 181n

Allison, Dorothy, 152

American Dream, 13–4, 100–1,
    106, 109–10, 114, 128–9, 138,
    165–6

Andrews, William, 38, 150

Anzaldua, Gloria, 5, 7, 42–5, 59,
    80, 117, 148–9, 165, 177–8n,
    180–1n

autonomy, 7, 8, 10, 13, 31, 43, 49,
    55, 62, 66, 72–3, 84–5, 89,
    91, 95, 101, 119, 121, 125,
    155, 161, 166
    female, women, 4, 6, 39, 49–50,
        51–2, 54, 77, 80–1, 120–1,
        160, 169

Avey Johnson, 9

Awkward, Michael, 90

Baker, Houston, 120

Bambara, Toni Cade, 29, 143

*Behind the Scenes. Or, Thirty Years a
    Slave, and Four Years in the
    White House,* 30, 36, 151, 155

Berlin, Ira, 57

Beyond, beyond, 4, 5, 14–5, 38–9,
    40, 47, 49, 50, 53, 59, 62–4,
    97, 109, 133, 139, 154, 165,
    155, 176–7n

Bhabha, Homi K., 5, 7–8, 15, 38,
    45–9, 51, 76, 83, 85, 165,
    176–8n, 181n

Bone, Robert A., 120

Borderlands La Frontera, 42–3

borders, 4–5, 9, 11–2, 14, 33,
    44–5, 73, 126, 146, 148,
    166–7, 173n
    See also boundaries, margins,
    crossing borders, 4, 7

boundaries, 1–5, 7–8, 11–2, 14, 33,
    43, 45, 61, 66–7, 72, 78, 84,
    87, 148, 152, 161, 170, 178n

Brooks, Kristina, 179, 182

Butler, Octavia, 3, 10, 144–63,
    166, 181n

Carby, Hazel, 151, 153

center, 2, 9, 12, 33–4, 37–8, 45–7,
    73, 80, 99, 116, 119, 131,
    167, 171
    See also female

Chancy, Myriam J. A., 171

change, 2–10, 12–4, 16–7, 20, 22,
    25–6, 28–32, 35, 38, 40, 43,
    44–5, 48–50, 52, 58–9, 62–3,
    66–7, 71, 75, 79, 84–7, 89
    92–3, 96, 118, 122, 127,
    143–4, 155, 162, 168, 176n

Christian, Barbara, 9, 28–9, 53, 66,
    93, 94–5, 102, 105, 110,
    112–4, 120, 123–4, 126

Collins, Patricia Hill, 7, 15, 16,
    20–5, 30, 36, 39, 52, 55, 61,
    87–8, 95, 158, 169, 174n

The Color Purple, 90

consciousness, 3–12, 14, 35,
    125–6, 138, 169, 173n
    changed, 29–30, 44–5, 97, 146

consciousness—*Continued*
  double, 9, 14, 43, 59, 176n, 177n
  female, black, 3–12, 14–5, 26,
    29, 31–3, 38, 40, 47–9, 52,
    62–3, 65, 67, 74, 87, 91–2,
    95–7, 101–2, 102, 117–19,
    136, 141, 146, 166–7, 170,
    173n, 174n, 176n
  mestiza, 42–4
Consciousness, stage, 9, 14, 32,
    34–6
Contending Forces, 1, 3, 54–81,
    120–21, 125, 166–67,
    173n, 178n
Cooper, Anna Julia, 18, 27–8,
    61, 160
Corner, Tawana Chimney, 28
crossings, 148, 166
Crossley, Robert, 148, 153, 157–8,
Cult of True Womanhood, 8,
    18–20, 70, 75, 78, 81, 87,
    178–9n

Davies, Carole Boyce, 165, 178, 181n
Davis, Thadious M., 106
DeLamotte, Eugenia, 1, 118, 126,
    127, 133, 135–6, 140, 146, 173n
Douglass, Frederick, 42, 150
DuBois, W. E. B., 43, 177n
DuCille, Ann, 56, 119–20, 179–80n

enslavement, 2, 4–6, 8, 10, 15, 19,
    35, 54, 84, 148, 151, 166, 168
Ethnic Notions, 17, 185

female,
  center, 8, 9–13, 15, 31, 38, 46,
    49, 52–4, 56, 63, 65–6, 68,
    72, 76–7, 81, 84–6, 89–90,
    92, 140, 168–9, 171
  "erotic," 93, 96, 166, 175n
  object, 4, 6, 13–4, 20, 24–5,
    41–2, 44, 52, 58, 77, 80, 86–7,
    90, 92, 98, 107, 110, 124, 127,
    137, 141, 157, 175n
  oppression, 1–3, 5, 27, 48, 174n

power, 32, 127–8
psyche, 5, 24, 31, 49, 58, 62–3,
    67, 71, 73–4, 76–7, 80–1, 84,
    87, 92, 118, 123, 125–6,
    134, 137–9, 160, 166, 169,
    179n, 180n
sexuality, 14, 16–7, 20, 23–4, 30,
    55, 66, 71, 79, 88, 114, 119,
    160, 166, 175n, 180n
slave, *See also* slavery
subjectivity, 4–15, 25, 31, 33–4,
    41–2, 49, 56, 61, 63–5, 68, 72,
    83–6, 90, 107, 115, 119–20,
    125, 133, 163, 165, 167–9,
    173, 178–80n
feminist, black, 11, 37–8, 51, 59,
    86, 175n, 177n
flight, 9, 34, 37–8, 85, 111, 165–6
Foster, Francis Smith, 152, 160
Fulton, DoVeanna S., 22, 24, 30,
    37, 175n

"The Gilded Six–Bits", 23, 125, 175n,
Gilkes, Cheryl Townsend, 27
Gone With the Wind, 15–7, 174n
Green, Renee, 47–8
Griffin, Farah Jasmine, 86

Harper, Frances Ellen Watkins, 30,
    55, 169
healing, 52, 59, 76–7, 80–1, 118,
    126, 134, 137
hegemony, 4–6, 12, 14, 16, 20, 27,
    31, 33, 42–3, 45–6, 67, 78, 84,
    90–2, 96, 98–102, 109, 111,
    113–5, 130, 139, 145, 153,
    166–9, 181
  hegemonic, 6, 10–1, 13–4, 21–2,
    24, 27, 33, 52, 62, 96, 98, 111,
    161, 163, 165–6, 180n
Heidegger, Marti, 11
Henderson, Mae Gwendolyn, 6, 173
history, 40, 42–5, 52, 64, 84,
    118–9, 133, 147, 158
  family, 133
  self, 131, 162

home, 7, 171

hooks, bell, 1–3, 7, 11–2, 14, 20,
    31, 36, 40, 52, 57–8, 83–4,
    86, 92, 95, 97, 107, 115, 140,
    142, 166, 173n

Hopkins, Pauline E., 8–9, 51–2,
    56–60, 62, 63, 65, 67, 69–76,
    78–79, 81, 120–124

Hurston, Zora Neale Hurston, 23,
    4, 34, 55, 62, 88, 123–5, 158

identity, 23, 25, 35, 37, 40, 42–4,
    47–8, 51, 59–60, 76–80, 131,
    133, 148, 167, 169, 180n
  cultural, 180n
  dual, 43
  female, 4–5, 7, 9, 13, 27, 30, 43,
    50–1, 55, 65–9, 106, 108, 111,
    119–20, 123, 134, 166
  formation, 35, 40
  mestiza, 44–5, 180n

Iola Leroy, or Shadows Uplifted,
    55, 186

Image, 5, 8, 15–6, 18, 20–3, 27,
    30, 36, 39, 49, 56, 86, 98, 121,
    161, 174n
  See also Jezebel, 20

Imitation of Life, 174n, 186

Incidents in the Life of a Slave Girl,
    19, 26, 36, 53, 160

Innocence, 9, 34, 143

intercessory, 132

Jackson, Mattie, 40

Jacobs, Harriet, 19, 34, 35, 41,
    54, 149

jezebel, 15, 20, 174–5n

journey, 35, 37, 95, 96, 111, 131,
    138–9, 146, 150, 163

Keckley, Elizabeth, 30, 36–9, 151,
    153, 155

Kindred, 3, 10, 147–49, 151–53,
    155, 157, 159–61, 163,
    166, 181n

knowledge, 36

erotic, 31–2

female, 44–5, 90, 92–3, 96,
    100–1

self, 6, 8, 13, 23, 25, 31, 35,
    55–6, 79, 112–3, 167

Larsen, Nella, 9, 13, 23, 48, 62, 84,
    86–7, 90, 92–3, 101–2, 105–6,
    111, 114, 117, 122–3, 124,
    169, 180

location, 2–13, 15, 33, 38, 40,
    46–54, 56–9, 61–7, 84–90,
    92, 95, 97, 106, 112, 114–5,
    117–9, 129, 138, 149, 166,
    168, 170
  female–centered, 15, 90, 140

The Location of Culture, 177n

Lorde, Audre, 6–7, 12, 14, 28–9,
    32–2, 34, 38, 39, 42, 50 58,
    61–2, 67, 75, 89–91, 96, 106,
    119, 127, 158, 175n

Mammy, 16–17, 174n

mammy, 15–8, 20–1, 158, 174n

marginalization, marginality, 5, 35,
    51, 77, 84, 86, 169

margins, 11–2, 14, 33, 45, 71,
    98, 100–1, 114, 146, 166–7,
    173n, 178n

marriage, 19, 21, 23, 30, 54, 70,
    80, 102, 108, 119–21, 123–5,
    127–9, 132, 157, 169–70,
    174n, 179n, 180n

Marshall, Paule, 53, 117–9, 123,
    125–30, 136–41, 145,
    179–80n

Massey, Doreen, 73, 167

materialism, 106, 108, 118–9,
    122–3, 125–7, 129, 135–6
  materiality, 23, 77, 106, 108,
    118–9, 123, 128–30, 136, 142

McCullough, Kate, 71, 74

McDowell, Deborah, 162

memory, 78, 126, 142

mestiza, 43–45, 76, 170, 177n, 180n
  New Mestiza, 7–8, 42–4, 180n

movement, 4–6, 7–8, 15, 23,
    31–3m 39–40, 43, 45, 47–9,
    81m 111m 119, 123–4, 126,
    165, 168–9, 173n, 177n
Morrison, Toni, 89, 170
Myles, Lynette D., 24, 175n

Nakagawa, Chiho, 168
narrative, 125, 152
    of enslavement, 84, 149, 151, 166
    female, 2–10, 18, 30, 34–5, 40, 52,
        54, 102, 126, 150–1, 160, 168
    neo-slave, 149, 162, 181n
    slave, 30, 35, 42, 150–2, 160,
        162, 179n
Narrative of Sojourner Truth, 30, 189
nepantlera, 148–9
New Mestiza, 5, 180n
    consciousness, 43
New Negro, 179n

oppression,
    See also female oppression,
Other, 16, 52, 54, 64, 87, 89, 112,
    135, 177n
    otherness, 6, 33, 46, 49, 64, 87

Parma, Pratibha, 51, 178n
Passing, 23, 48, 76, 122–23,
    169, 180n,
    See also Quicksand
Peterson, Carla L., 173n,
Petry, Ann, 84, 92, 97–8, 101–5,
    110, 113–4
Pettis, Joyce, 101, 137, 145
Picquet, Louisa, 18–9
places,
    See also location, space
    transitory, 49, 67n, 75, 80, 86
Power, 2, 12, 16, 22, 25, 61, 74,
    96, 129, 156, 162
    See also erotic
Praisesong for the Widow, 3, 9,
    117–19, 121, 123, 125–7, 129,
    131, 133, 135, 139, 141, 143,
    145–6, 176n, 179n

Prince, Mary, 24, 40
psyche, 179n,
    female 5, 13, 49, 58, 62, 73, 118,
        126, 131, 160, 169, 179n, 180n
    fractured, 134, 138, 166, 180n
purge, 29, 137, 141–2, 166
    purging, 137, 141–2, 145, 166,
        176n, 180n

Quashie, Kevin Everod, 64, 65,
    178n
Quicksand, 99–103, 105–7, 109,
    111, 113, 115, 117–18, 122–3,
    165, 178–9, 187–8
    See also Passing

rape, 19, 24, 36, 69, 71, 76, 151, 161,
rebelliousness, 9
    stage of, 34, 37
recovery, 7, 29, 44, 62, 78, 137,
    142, 162, 166, 180n
Re-entry, *also* Materialization, 34,
    39, 162
    Return, 62, 78, 131, 137, 166,
        177n, 181n
    stage of 37
resistance, 2–4, 6, 12, 14, 31, 37,
    52, 55, 58, 75, 84, 86, 89, 95,
    125, 156, 160, 162, 171
Robertson, James O., 101
roots, 131
    See also history
Royster, Jacqueline Jones, 41, 66
Rushdy, Ashraf H. A., 181

Saldivar–Hull, Sonia, 43, 45
Sapphire, 15, 20, 23,
Sappho, 8, 53, 59–78, `63, 168
self, 1–2, 5–10, 38, 42, 45, 106, 189n
    fractured, 139–40,
    self–definition, 5, 7, 25, 38–9,
        46, 49, 52, 54–6, 61–2, 78, 89,
        99, 170, 177n
    self–hood, 3, 38, 42, 47,–8, 51,
        63, 64–6, 84–7, 89, 106, 150
    self–sufficiency, 15, 156

sexual,
  assault, 18, 31, 36, 41
  sexuality, 16–8, 23–4, 69, 71,
    166, *See also* female
Shange, Ntozake, 30, 143
site, 2–4, 67, 114, 141, 162, 167, 173
  transitory, 51–2, 67, 73, 76, 81,
    85–6
slave, 16–7, 40, 56, 160
  See also female
slavery, 18–20, 22, 25, 150,
    152–3, 181
society,
  See also hegemony
space, 1–9, 12–5, 33, 39, 51, 66
  See also place
  in-between, 47, 166
  intervening, 46–7, 76–7, 163, 176n
  liminal, 48
  safe, 6–7, 14, 33, 36, 38–40, 52,
    56, 58, 65, 75, 84–6, 89, 116,
    165–6, 169–70
  social construct, 167
stereotype, 6, 15, 21, 24, 53, 104,
    114, 175n
  image 8, 16–7
Stewart, Maria W., 2, 25–6, 60, 156
The Street, 3, 9, 13, 32, 48, 83–5,
    87, 89–93, 95, 97, 99, 101–7,
    109, 111, 113–5, 118, 165,
    178, 187–8
subject, 49
subjectivity, 4–11, 13–5, 23, 41–2,
    44, 47, 49, 56, 61–3, 78, 80,
    83–6, 89–90, 107, 114, 133,
    138, 171
  female, 4–8, 10, 13, 15, 25, 31,
    33–4, 49, 56, 61, 63–5, 68,
    72, 84, 90, 115, 119, 125, 163,
    167, 169, 178n, 180n
  subject hood, 49

Tate, Claudia, 3, 7, 11, 13, 27

Their Eyes Were Watching God, 2,
    21, 30, 34, 62, 124–5, 146,
    186, 189
theory, feminist 177n
theory, theorizing, 28, 177n, 178n
Third Space, 5, 7–8, 15, 33, 37, 40,
    45–50, 76, 83, 85, 87, 90, 92,
    96–7, 106, 111–2, 115, 141,
    167, 170–1, 176–7, 176–7n
transformation, 2, 6–10, 12, 29, 43,
    49, 51, 61, 75–7, 84–5, 87, 89,
    92, 98, 101, 118–9, 144, 163,
    165, 167–8
Transient Woman, 5–10, 15,
    33–40, 42–3, 47, 59, 76–7, 81,
    85, 90–2, 95–6, 98, 106, 117,
    141, 160, 162–3, 167, 169–70,
    176–8n
Truth, Sojourner, 17, 30, 37
Turner, Nat, 40

A Voice from the South, 27

Walker, Alice, 21, 66, 90, 126,
    175–6n
Weiner, Marli F., 19
Welter, Barbara, 178–9n
Washington, Mary Helen, 38,
    88, 146
white, whiteness, 180n
  center, 131m 141m 174n
wholeness, female 130, 131, 138
Williams, Patricia J., 100, 165
Willis Susan, 131, 137, 141
womanhood, 6, 9, 20, 23, 25–6,
    28–9, 39, 47, 49, 54–5, 59, 62,
    69, 81 173n,
  black, 26, 38
women, writers, 5, 15, 21, 56, 105,
    118, 121, 125, 124, 138, 140,
    160, 169, 180n

The Young and the Restless, 174n